Aladdin Ayesh

Essential UML™ *fast*

Using SELECT Use Case Tool for Rapid Applications Development

Springer

Aladdin Ayesh, BSc, MSc
Department of Computing Information Sciences, De Montfort University,
The Gateway, Leicester LE1 9BH

Series Editor
John Cowell, BSc (Hons), MPhil, PhD
Department of Computer Science, De Montfort University, The Gateway,
Leicester LE1 9BH

British Library Cataloguing in Publication Data
A catalogue record for this book is available from the British Library.

Library of Congress Cataloging-in-Publication Data
Ayesh, Aladdin, 1972-
Essential UML fast : using SELECT use case tool for rapid applications development /
Aladdin Ayesh.
p. cm. – (Essential series)
Includes bibliographical references and index.
ISBN 1-85233-413-4 (alk. paper)
1. Application software—Development. 2. UML (Computer science) I. Title. II.
Essential series (Springer-Verlag)
QA76.76.A65 A94 2002
005.1—dc21
2002021724

Essential series ISSN 1439-975X
ISBN 1-85233-413-4 Springer-Verlag London Berlin Heidelberg
a member of BertelsmannSpringer Science+Business Media GmbH
http://www.springer.co.uk

© Springer-Verlag London Limited 2002
Printed in Great Britain

Typesetting: Mac Style Ltd, Scarborough, N. Yorkshire
Printed and bound at The Cromwell Press, Trowbridge, Wiltshire
34/3830-543210 Printed on acid-free paper SPIN 10789834

Essential Series

Springer

London
Berlin
Heidelberg
New York
Barcelona
Hong Kong
Milan
Paris
Singapore
Tokyo

Contents

Chapter 1

Introduction

Introduction

Object-oriented (OO) technology is taking the applications development world by storm as large-scale systems increasingly rely on this technology as the core of their analysis and design. OO technology has also benefited from the rapid development of the Internet. World Wide Web browsers nowadays deploy OO concepts in handling and transmitting media objects. For example, DHTML, which is used to implement interactive web sites, relies on the Document Object Model (DOM). DOM is an object-oriented model that allows us to handle HTML tags and other web page components, such as images, as objects. These objects can then be manipulated through events and methods to achieve interactivity for the site. The development of large-scale applications, such as the Windows operating system and Internet applications and browsers, made OO technology vital for any serious application development.

In this chapter we will look at some essential topics related to systems analysis and design and the changes in system development approaches. These topics include:

- Analysis and design approaches
- Rapid Application Development
- CASE tools
- Use case driven approaches.

Analysis and design approaches

Analysis and design are the first steps in building any system or application. We do these two processes, consciously or unconsciously, every time we implement an application. The success or failure of a system usually depends on the quality of its analysis and design. As a result, the search for appropriate, sufficient and effective approaches to analysis and design has no end and neither does the list of analysis and design approaches.

Analysis and design approaches vary greatly depending on the application which we are trying to analyze and implement. As an example, the specification of a large database information system will be very different to the analysis and design of a new operating system, while operating systems may have different requirements depending on whether they are for parallel computing, networks or a stand-alone machine.

Rapid Application Development

Rapid Application Development (RAD) is a popular approach. It benefits from the principles of prototyping, which we will look at in the next chapter where we discuss application life cycles. The RAD approach assigns a time limit to each task or subsystem. This time limit, unlike in traditional development methods, is rigid. This inflexibility in time, which could give rise to problems, is combined with flexibility in defining system requirements and specifications. There are two types of specifications:

- Essential requirements are the core requirements which the system must provide, so system developers focus on these requirements first.
- Desired requirements, on the other hand, are not critical so developers do not deal with them unless sufficient time is available.

This rigid time technique is usually referred to as "time boxing".

CASE tools, approaches and methodologies

CASE tools are tools that assist with software design. They are based on one or more modelling languages developed to help designers to model their design. CASE tools usually provide a visual representation of software architecture and control flow. Some examples of CASE tools are SELECT Enterprise and the Rational Rose modelling products.

An approach is a general philosophy or standpoint we may take to systems development. Methodologies usually conform to one approach or another. For example, Larman and Jacobson methodologies conform to the object-oriented approach. The use case driven approach, which is closely related to the OO approach, relies heavily on the deployment of Unified Modelling Language (UML) use case diagrams to represent end user requirements. This approach is employed in many methodologies, such as Jacobson methodology, and is particularly popular with information systems practitioners.

Who is this book for?

This book is for system developers at all levels: for professional analysts and designers who like to move quickly into application development using CASE tools, and for newcomers to systems development. This book provides a quick way to understand the modelling language widely used in RAD approaches. UML provides a graphical means of quickly analyzing, designing and modelling systems with prototyping in mind. In addition, this book provides a fast way to learn how to use one of the most widely used CASE tools, SELECT Enterprise, that implements UML.

The basics of systems modelling and systems life cycles are presented in Chapter 2. A good understanding of the different approaches to systems is important for us to understand the different analysis and design approaches and to appreciate the strengths of UML and OO technology; this is especially important for newcomers to analysis and design. Chapter 3 follows this with an introduction to the object-oriented approach, which is important if you have no previous experience with OO technology.

What do you need to use UML?

This book presents UML through the use of SELECT Enterprise version 6. However, it can also be used with SELECT Enterprise version 5, other CASE tools, such as Rational Rose, or graphical software, such as Visio. You need to work with one of these software products as you read the book.

In addition to the software, you need some basic understanding of the development process. If you have previous experience in programming or software development then you can choose which part of the book to start with. If you do not have such experience, the first three chapters will give you the background you need to work on the rest of the book and to analyze and design systems *fast*.

Chapter 2

Introduction to Modelling

Introduction

Some of the most unpopular pieces of software are those which meet the designer's specification and do not crash, but which do not do what the user wants. This unhappy and far too common situation occurs as a result of a failure in the design process. Modelling the system to be implemented and ensuring that it meets the customers' need is a vital part of producing systems that not only work efficiently but also are what the user wants. In this chapter we will look at:

- Business modelling
- Structure vs behaviour
- Life cycles
- UML

Business modelling

An important distinction can be drawn between applications that target a particular organization or business and generic applications that can be used by wide group of users. As an example, MS Word is a generic application that can be used by any organization or business while a company database is a specific application – or set of applications – developed to meet the company requirements and needs. The difference between these two types of applications greatly affects the process of analysis and design.

If we are building a business-specific product, we have to look carefully at the business organization and how it deals with the problem at hand. There may be some sort of manual or computerized system in place and we need to understand and model the correct processes before we begin to design the new system. We call this **business modelling**. As part of the process of business modelling, we may present suggestions that modify or adapt the existing practices for more efficient implementation. In a new company, the business model should reflect the management plan.

If we are developing a generic application, there is no need for a business model and we may need an open system design. Open systems design is a specialized subject with more specific and complicated issues. Therefore, open systems are not specifically covered in this book. Instead we will keep to a generic use of UML for analysis and design.

Structure vs behaviour

There are two main characteristics of any system that we are interested in knowing about and modelling: the structure of the system and how it behaves. Structural modelling provides a view of the relationships between different entities, sections, subsystems and parts of the system. The structure of a system varies depending on what we are trying to achieve with that system. Usually, in business applications, the system structure is dominated by the organizational structure of that business.

Behavioural modelling provides a view of the functionality and behaviour of the system in response to actions and events. Behavioural modelling is important to ensure the correctness of the system in response to the environmental changes. In particular, behavioural modelling can make the difference between a user-friendly system and one which the users hate. In other words, it can make the difference between the system being acceptable or unacceptable.

Storyboarding

Storyboarding is becoming an important part of modern system development approaches, especially with use case driven methods. The original use of storyboarding was in movie making and cartoon design.

The concept of storyboarding involves the presentation of changes, events or states of the system as frames with relationships that link these frames together in a story-telling format. This concept is used in object-oriented analysis and design when defining use cases and designing interfaces.

Use cases (Chapter 5) represent the interaction between groups of users that are represented as actors, for example, managers. Each use case tells a story of events, or a sequence of processes, which lead to a task to be completed, for example, booking a room in a hotel booking system. Similarly, some design models such as collaboration diagrams (Chapter 7) and state transition diagrams (Chapter 8) can be viewed as storyboards of class activities.

Designing user interface objects and screens relies on storyboarding as an essential development tool.

Hierarchies

Hierarchies are important in modelling organizations and business processes. These hierarchies can take several forms, such as part-of and parent-child.

Life cycles

Each software development project has a life cycle that stretches from its inception until the software is no longer used. A life cycle consists of the steps that software engineers follow during the preparation, construction and maintenance of the software. These steps may vary depending on the analysis and design concepts that are used, the complexity of the project and the technology used. The concepts of structural and object-oriented analysis and design will be discussed in the next chapter. In this section, we will focus on a variety of life cycles.

Traditional life cycle

The traditional or classic life cycle is often referred to as the waterfall model (Figure 2.1). This is the simplest life cycle with straightforward steps. It is often used with traditional software development methodologies such as Structured Systems Analysis and Design Method (SSADM).

In structured methodologies, the different processes of analysis and design are clearly separated and map to the steps of the traditional life cycle. The activities of each step, e.g. requirements gathering, have to be completed before moving to the next step. As a result, the traditional life cycle lacks the flexibility that other life cycles provide; therefore it is not commonly used in object-oriented software development.

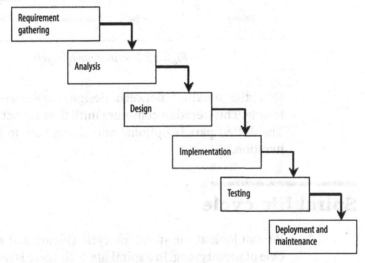

Figure 2.1 Waterfall life cycle.

Prototype life cycle

The prototype life cycle (Figure 2.2) presents a concept that is not found in the waterfall life cycle. The idea of prototyping is to quickly build a simplified version of the system so the user can gain a sense of what the final system will be like at an early stage in its development. This enables better communication between the user and designer; it also enables the designer to review the specifications and requirements analysis.

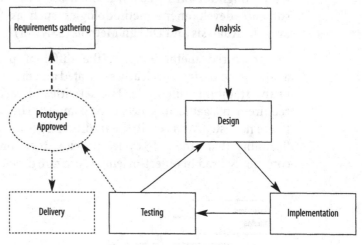

Figure 2.2 *Prototype life cycle*

Note the iteration between design, implementation and testing. This iteration continues until the product is finished. The dotted part is optional and shows how to finalize the iteration.

Spiral life cycle

We can look at the spiral life cycle (Figure 2.3) as a special case of prototyping. In a spiral life cycle there is no end point: the review and development keeps on going until the system expires. In this life cycle there are usually four phases:

- Planning: this may include risk assessment, visibility studies and requirements gathering
- Analysis
- Development: this is usually done in a prototyping fashion

- Evaluation: this usually includes user assessment and feedback.

Figure 2.3 *Spiral life cycle*

V-shaped life cycle

The V-shaped life cycle (Figure 2.4) can be seen as the result of cross-over between the prototype and waterfall life cycles.

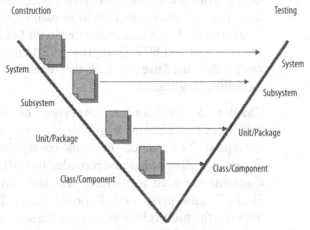

Figure 2.4 *V-shaped life cycle.*

We can add the steps of analysis, design and implementation as horizontal lines as we move from system to class. During the system phase, requirements are gathered, analyzed and the general system architecture is identified. Design starts by identifying subsystems and units. At this stage, requirements are turned into functional and non-functional specifications. At the class level, the actual coding of the system starts and then the testing. Notice that the testing phase operates on the components in reverse order to that of development.

Unified Modelling Language

Unified Modelling Language (UML) is a combination of analysis and design models that provide software developers with formal ways to communicate both with the users and with each other. UML is an object-oriented modelling language. In other words, UML supports object-oriented principles and provides the modelling diagrams that are needed to develop software using these principles.

The main advantage of UML over other object-oriented modelling languages is the wide range of tools available. These tools provide good coverage of all software development steps from requirements gathering to implementation. This book focuses on UML as it is implemented in the SELECT Enterprise use case tool. SELECT Enterprise and Rational Rose are the most widely-used use case tools that deploy UML as their base modelling language.

Chapter 3 provides an overview of object-oriented principles and Chapter 4 provides an overview of SELECT Enterprise. The rest of the book covers the analysis and design modelling diagrams provided by UML. Most of these diagrams are used in more or less the same way in both SELECT Enterprise and Rational Rose. The difference between the tools is in how you use the software rather than in the deployed UML diagrams.

CASE tools

There are several commercially available software tools to help software engineers with their work. These tools are usually associated with an analysis and design methodology, technique or modelling language. For example, SELECT Enterprise supports Unified Modelling Language and Rational Rose supports the unified modelling methodology, which is based on UML. Generally, use case tools are linked to modelling languages that provide a visual expression of analysis and design and the use case tool software provides some of the following:

- Requirements gathering and analysis modelling tools – usually textual or diagrammatic use cases
- Functional and non-functional analysis diagrams
- Internal design diagrams
- External or interface design diagrams
- Architectural design diagrams.

The combination and emphasis of the diagrams will depend on the modelling language that the use case tool supports. For example, use case tools that support structured analysis and design techniques will focus on data flow while the ones that support real-time systems will focus on processes and time constraints.

How to choose CASE tools

There are several CASE tools on the market that enable you to document your analysis and design models. The wide range of software sometimes makes the choice difficult. If you are choosing a new CASE tool you need to consider the following questions:

- Does the software support the approach you are using or like to use?
- Does the software have an integration mechanism that links models and checks their consistency? If so, which methodologies does this mechanism support?

- Does the software enable all stages of software development? Does it have tools to convert models into a programming language?

If you are considering changing or updating your current CASE tool, you need to consider the following questions:

- Does your current software enable you to do the job properly?
- Is your current software fast enough for your requirements?
- Will the new software enable you to design systems any better? If so, do the benefits justify the cost?
- Does the new software gives better facilities and faster development?
- What is the cost of change in terms of training time and change of methodologies and techniques? Is it justified?

Usually, different tools are required if we are changing our approach or methodology. For example, if we are changing our approach from structured to object-oriented, then we have to choose CASE tools that supports this approach. We have to remember that the CASE tools are meant to assist in the process of software development and are not an end in themselves.

Chapter 3

Object-Oriented Technlogy

Introduction

Object-oriented technology (OOT) is increasingly important and has come to dominate the thinking of the modern software development community. Whether you are using Visual Basic, DHTML or Java you will find an understanding of object-oriented technology to be useful. In this chapter we will look at:

- Structured and object modelling
- Principles of object-oriented technology.

Structured modelling and object modelling

Most programmers who work with high-level third-generation programming languages, such as C and Pascal, usually follow structured design and coding principles.

The basic principle behind structured design is to divide the program into sub-sections, each of which does one or more operations. These sub-sections may be functions, procedures, or units: they are all a sequence of program statements. These units are associated with each other within a structure. In other words we may have a procedure, which may be divided into three units, each of which may then be divided into smaller units and so on. Figure 3.1 shows the general layout of a structured program.

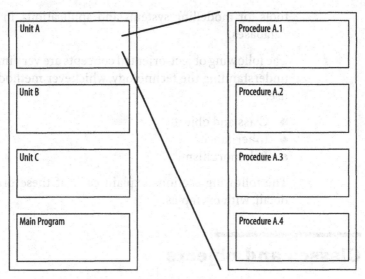

Figure 3.1 Structured programs.

A distinctive feature of structured programming is that the data structures are separated from the functions or procedures that apply to them. As a result, there is little control over data security in response to the access of procedures within the system. This is not so important an issue in stand-alone systems, however it is of extreme importance in distributed systems such as Internet databases.

Object-oriented modelling differs in principle and concept from structured modelling. The system is divided into objects, rather than sub-sections, and data and functions are brought together within an object, which is responsible for the safety of the data.

Concepts of object-oriented technology

Object-oriented systems rely on basic principles taken from object-oriented programming. Many object-oriented methodologies add to these principles to provide complete tools for modelling systems and applications, in particular databases.

The following object-oriented concepts are very important to understanding the technology, whichever methodology you use:

- Class and object
- Inheritance
- Polymorphism.

The following sections explain each of these principles in detail, with examples.

Classes and objects

Classes and objects are key concepts in object-oriented technology. A *class* is an abstract form that represents the structure and behaviour of a group of objects. Let us take as an example the people in a college. As shown in Figure 3.2, they may be grouped into classes such as students, teachers, assistants, administrators, and so on.

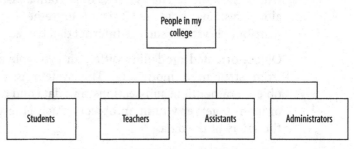

Figure 3.2 Objects grouped into classes.

We group objects to simplify or standardize our dealing with them. For example, we may say all students should study for 180 hours before graduating. As a result, if John is a student, he must study for 180 hours to graduate. *Students* is a class in which *John* is an object. Sometimes we may refer to *John* as an instance of the class *Students*. Classes in a system may be identified on the basis of the objects' jobs, departments, nature and so on. For example, the *Equipment* class in a company system may refer to all types of equipment, whether they are photocopiers, fax machines or computers.

In summary, a class is an abstract model of objects that share the same attributes and functionality. In some cases, a class may be divided into smaller classes, which are known as subclasses. For example, subclass of *Equipment* may group computers together and separate them from other types of equipment. This leads to the second principle of object-oriented technology: inheritance.

Inheritance and relationships

An object-oriented approach benefits from both object-oriented programming and relational database principles by linking classes and defining their relationships to each other. In modern object-oriented methodologies, classes can relate to each other by inheritance, relations similar to those in relational databases, or associations.

It is clear that all employees of a company will have similar data stored about them such as name, salary and so on. However, groups of employees will have different privileges and responsibilities within the company. Therefore we need different classes of the type *Employee* to represent the different groups of employee. Figure 3.3 shows an inheritance relationship between the *Employee* class and two types of employees, which are represented by the *Manager* and *Accountant* classes.

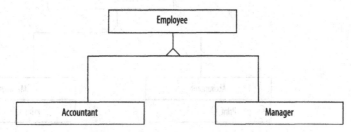

Figure 3.3 Inheritance relationship.

Notice that Figure 3.3 uses UML notation for modelling inheritance (a triangle connector). You can go back to Figure 3.2 and add the connecter to show the inheritance or class-subclass relationships on that diagram.

As object-oriented technology developed, new associations or relationships were introduced; some were influenced by relational databases, others by research into code reuse. The effect of these associations is reflected in the instantiation of classes. For an example, in an accounting system, we may have a *Customer* class and an *Account* class. The creation of an instance of the *Customer* class may lead to the creation of an *Account* instance that relates to the *Customer* instance. This means there is an association directed from the *Customer* class to the *Account* class, which may be labelled as *has*.

Polymorphism

In OO programming functions are referred to as methods. Polymorphism is the concept of using the same function (or method) name in more than one class. Polymorphism also relates to inheritance between classes.

Commonly when there is inheritance between classes, one or more methods may be written differently within two classes at the same level of the inheritance tree. For example, consider the Print function that is inherited from the *Employee* class by the *Accountant* and *Manager* classes, as shown in Figure 3.4.

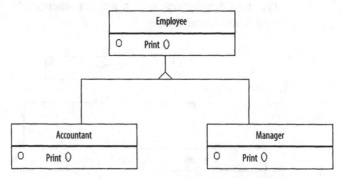

***Figure 3.4** Polymorphism of the Print method.*

Different data must be printed for the *Accountant* and *Manager* classes. This means that the Print method in *Accountant* is different from the Print method in *Manager* and both are different from the Print method in the *Employee* class. Here we would say there is polymorphism.

In addition, we may have two or more versions of the same function in one class. For example, we may have different Print methods within the Accountant class depending on the data of the accountant that we want to print. In this case, the different versions are distinguished from each other by their parameters, which are sometimes referred to as the "signature" of the function.

The other related term to polymorphism is overriding. If we look again at Figure 3.4, the Print method in *Manager* is inherited from *Employee*. However, we may decide to expand the Print method to fit the specifications of the *Manager* class. In this case we say we are overriding the Print method of *Employee*. This allows us to reuse and expand on the code written in the *Employee* class.

Introduction

SELECT Enterprise is a well-known CASE tool, which has been used by software developers for a long time. SELECT Enterprise is the object-oriented version of SELECT software. The current version of SELECT Enterprise (version 6) may seem to be a complicated piece of software. However when you become familiar with it you will appreciate its flexibility and excellent user interface. It also has several tools that make developing software a pleasure. To release all this potential you have to be patient and to understand the different components of SELECT Enterprise before starting to develop your project. In this chapter we will look at:

- Installing SELECT Enterprise
- Server-client components
- Using Enabler
- Starting SELECT Enterprise
- Errors you should avoid.

It is worth reading this chapter before you go any further even if you have used SELECT CASE tools before. Most common errors occur from the assumption that SELECT Enterprise versions 5 and 6 behave exactly in the same way.

Installing SELECT Enterprise

Installing SELECT Enterprise is an easy task but it requires patience. If you have a Pentium III, Celeron or better, with Windows 98 or Windows NT you should not have a problem. However, whatever your machine specifications, the installation process is somewhat time-consuming in comparison with other Windows software. You have to be patient during this process as any mistake may affect the running of SELECT Enterprise and may require the re-installation of the system.

Once your installation process has established the environment, you are prompted to select from a series of choices. SELECT Enterprise, in common with many new development tools, comes in two parts:

- Server applications, which reside on the server in a networked environment
- Client applications, which reside on the client machines.

If you are installing the system on a stand-alone machine, you must tell the installation process to install both the client and the server applications. You become, in that case, both the administrator and the user.

You will also be asked whether or not you will use your machine away from the network. You should answer "Yes" to this question if you are developing on a standalone machine, which you may use away from the office or college, detached from any network.

Using the Enabler

If you install SELECT Enterprise on a stand-alone machine, you are the administrator of the SELECT environment as well as the user. You administer SELECT Enterprise in the same manner, whether it is networked or stand-alone.

The Enabler or Repository Administrator is the SELECT Enterprise administration tool. It allows you to create repositories, initialise them and give access permissions. We can run the Enabler from the Tools menu of SELECT Enterprise or from the Start menu in Windows.

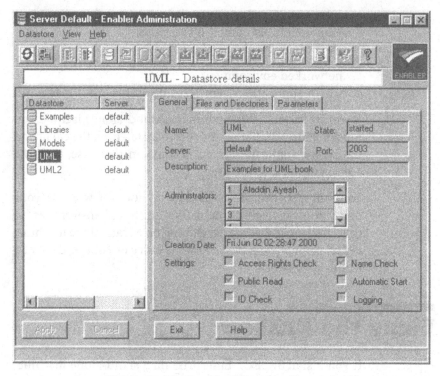

Figure 4.1 The Enabler administration tool.

Creating a new repository

Creating a new repository, or datastore, is like creating a new user account. Only administrators who are given the access rights can view and modify the repository. To create a new repository, go to the Datastore menu and then choose Create, as shown in Figure 4.2.

Administrators generally use the Enabler to close a datastore after use. Not doing so will destroy the datastore and it will require re-creation. However, you may often find that the Enabler manages to repair the damage, if you restart the damaged datastore using the Enabler.

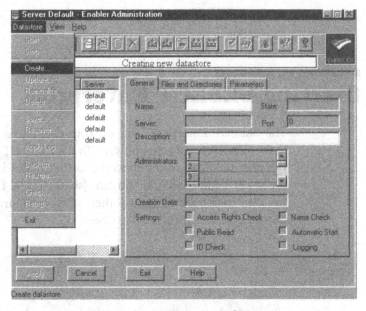

Figure 4.2 Creating a new datastore.

Creating a new model

Once you have installed SELECT Enterprise, two icons will appear on your desktop: SELECT Enterprise and SELECT Models. The SELECT Models icon is a shortcut folder that contains references to sample datastores and models that come with the package.

The datastores that you create using the Enabler must be referenced from this icon. To do that, open the SELECT Models folder and map to the new datastore by choosing the File | Map menu option.

There are two ways to create a new model:

● Open the SELECT Models folder, open the datastore within which you want to create the model and then choose the New Model menu option.

- Start SELECT Enterprise and use the `File | New Model` option.

Starting SELECT Enterprise

The SELECT Enterprise icon on your desktop is a shortcut to the SELECT Enterprise software. To start SELECT Enterprise, you may double-click on this icon or on one of the datastores in the SELECT Models folder. You can also run SELECT Enterprise from the Start menu like any other software. Figure 4.3 shows the SELECT Enterprise environment.

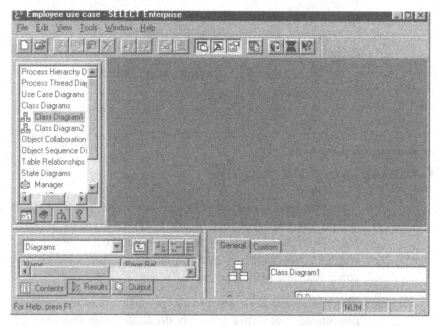

Figure 4.3 The SELECT Enterprise user interface.

SELECT Enterprise provides a visual modelling environment. If you have programmed in any other visual programming environment (such as Visual Basic or Access), you should be able to understand the SELECT Enterprise environment very easily. If you do not have such experience, here is a quick review of the important menus to get you going.

The File menu (see Figure 4.4) provides us with functions to create new models and diagrams. It also provides useful tools for printing.

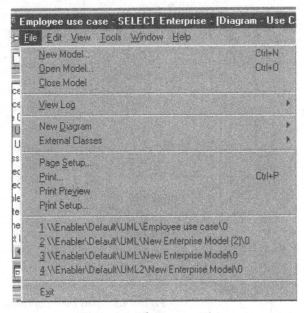

Figure 4.4 *File menu options.*

The Tools menu (see Figure 4.5) provides us with many useful tools and extras, some of which we discuss in Chapter 9. This menu includes the Repository Administrator option, which starts the Enabler.

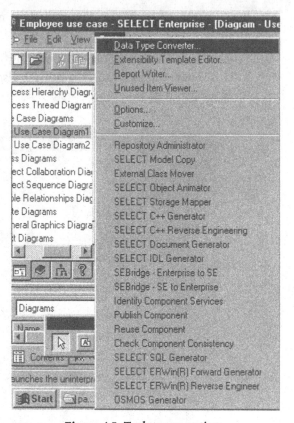

Figure 4.5 Tools menu options.

Common errors

Users of SELECT Enterprise version 6 often make errors associated with the concept of the server-client model and the associated components.

A common error is to attempt to rush the installation. If you do so, the installation may not be successful and several components may not work properly. During the installation, the whole system may pause as if the system has crashed. However, some of the activities take a long time and the system may not have crashed: observe the hard disk light for any activity and be patient.

If you are installing the software on a standalone machine, ensure that you do not enforce the use of an external server. The best way to do so is to rely on the default during the installation. If you specify the use of an external server, the Enabler may not work properly and you may be asked frequently for a server address to connect to. If this happens, reinstall the software with the correct settings.

Record your settings and the choices you make during installation. You may need to consider changing your selected settings, when you reinstall the software, if the software does not work with the initially chosen settings.

Another common error is attempting to shut down the computer without closing the datastores. This will damage the open datastores. You should close all datastores using the Enabler, before shutting the computer down. If the computer crashes, it is very likely the open datastores will be damaged and you should not attempt to open the damaged datastores from SELECT Enterprise. Instead, try to start them from Enabler. Enabler will display a message informing you that the datastore is damaged; choose the option to repair the datastore. The Enabler seems to recover the damaged datastores almost all the time. It took me some time to discover this option after losing my datastores several times.

If you are upgrading a model from SELECT Enterprise version 5.1 to version 6.0 some state diagrams may be affected. As a result you may find that some sub-states are displayed differently. This book refers to SELECT Enterprise version 6. The good news is that UML is a standard modelling language, so what we cover in this book applies with minor variations to any SELECT Enterprise software version or indeed any CASE tool that is based on UML.

Chapter 5

Use Case

Introduction

The first step of analysis and design is to define the requirements of the system. There are several ways to do so, however the formal method in UML is the use case. We have discussed use-case driven approaches and CASE tools in previous chapters. In this chapter we will look at:

- What is a use case?
- Creating use cases
- Linking use cases
- Abstract and detailed use cases
- Requirements gathering and analysis

What is a use case?

Use cases were introduced by Jacobson in 1992. They model how the system is going to be used in a given context and give an overall picture of the system from a user's point of view. The main purpose of use cases is to capture and communicate requirements.

A use case diagram details the ways in which a system can be used and the interaction of objects in that system. This type of modelling is now widely accepted as being the best means of establishing user requirements and of feeding those requirements into object-oriented analysis. The use case model provides an efficient communication mechanism between users and developers.

Diagrammatic views

Diagrammatic views (see Figure 5.1) are the most popular form of use case. Visually modelling the processes makes it easier for the designer and the user to exchange ideas regarding the process.

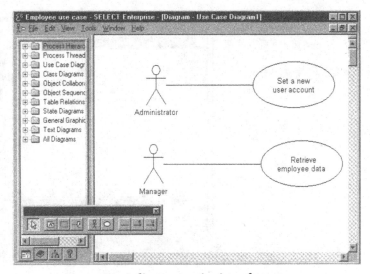

Figure 5.1 *A diagrammatic view of a use case.*

Figure 5.1 shows two actors called *Manager* and *Administrator*. We will describe actors in more detail later on in this chapter.

Textual views

Textual views (see Figure 5.2) are an alternative way of describing use cases. Text is used instead of visual modelling. Although there are no precise standards with which one has to comply, there are general practice guidelines for using textual views.

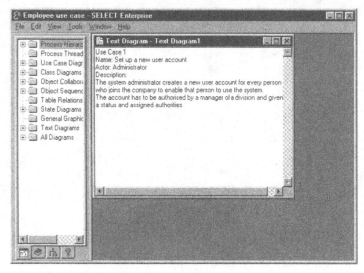

Figure 5.2 A textual view of a use case.

In Figure 5.2, the use case is described by the following pieces of information:

- Number
- Name
- Actor
- Description

Each use case may have one or more actors and may be associated with other use cases. The description should include instructional statements in a story-like sequence that tell what the use case is about.

Creating a use case

Systems analysts and designers usually prefer diagrammatic use cases because they are easier to use in communication both with the users and experts of any given system especially at the early stage of system analysis process.

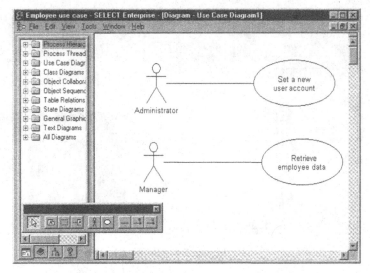

Figure 5.3 Creating use cases using the toolbox.

A use case consists of an actor, a process and a link between the actor and the process.

We have to be clear about the meaning of the term actor: it does not represent a particular user. It rather represents a group of users or the role of these users. For example in Figure 5.3 we see the actor *Manager* which refers to the role played by a user.

Adding an actor

I find it easier to start the use case from the perspective of the actor. Defining who is using or has the right to access the process is usually helpful and a good starting point in communicating with the potential users of the system under development.

To add an actor, right-click on the use case diagram window and select Add | Actor (see Figure 5.4).

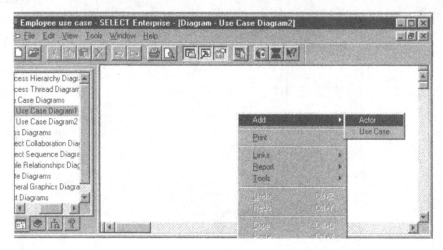

Figure 5.4 *Adding an actor.*

Another drop down menu appears (see Figure 5.5) giving a list of existing actors and the choice of adding new actor.

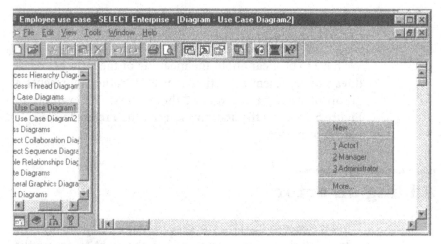

Figure 5.5 *Adding new or previously-defined actors.*

If this is your first actor, the list will be empty. If you choose to add a new actor, it is added to the diagram with a default name (see *Actor2* in Figure 5.6). It is good practice to change the name of the actor to a meaningful name, such as *Manager* or *Accountant*.

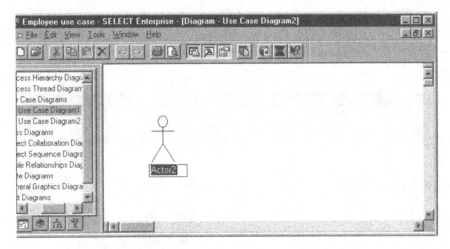

Figure 5.6 *Renaming a new actor.*

An alternative way to add an actor is to click on the `Actor` icon in the use case toolbox and then click inside the use case diagram window.

Adding a process

Processes are an important part of the use case; when we add a new process, we effectively add a use case.

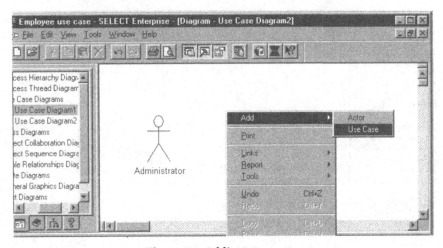

Figure 5.7 *Adding a use case.*

The steps to add a process are very similar to those for adding an actor. This time we choose Use Case from the drop down menu, as shown in Figures 5.7 and 5.8.

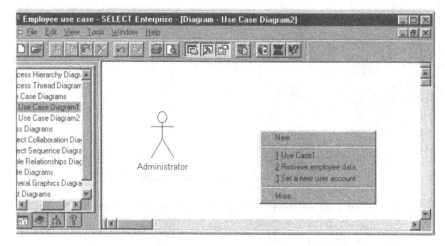

Figure 5.8 *Adding new or existing use cases.*

Figure 5.9 shows the new use case. It is good practice, when we add a new use case, to give it a meaningful name to distinguish it from other use cases in our model.

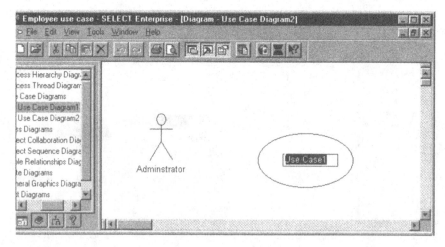

Figure 5.9 *A new use case.*

Linking an actor to a process

The next step after adding an actor and a use case (process) is to add a link between the two. Adding a link is done in similar way to adding the actor and the process. In Figure 5.10, the toolbox is used to add the link between the actor and the use case.

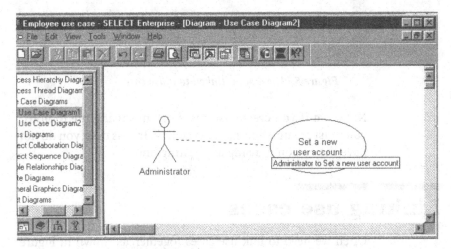

Figure 5.10 Adding a link using the toolbox.

Figure 5.11 shows that the actor *Administrator* is using the use case *Set a new user account*.

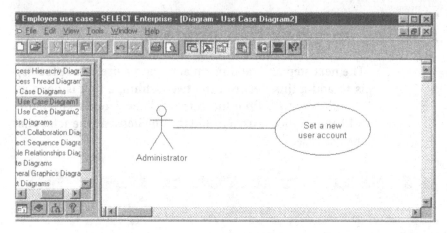

Figure 5.11 An actor linked to a use case.

Note that if you create use cases or links using the toolbox, you must create a new use case or link. In this case, you do not have the option of using an existing one.

Linking use cases

Often we need to link use cases together, as shown in Figure 5.12. There are three types of links between use cases that we can use. We used the ordinary link to link the actor to the use case.

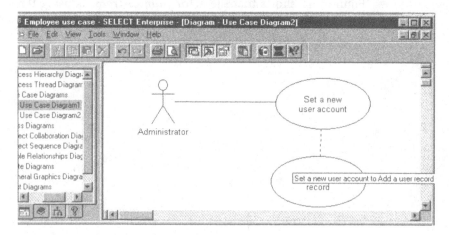

Figure 5.12 Linking two use cases.

The second type of link extends a use case by another use case. For example, in Figure 5.13, the process of Set a new user account extends the process of Add a user record. Effectively, the two processes become part of each other.

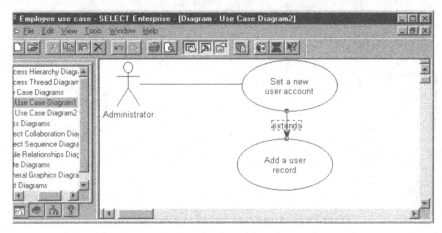

Figure 5.13 Adding an extends link.

The third type of link is the use link, which contrasts with the extends link. The use case uses or employs another use case as part of its overall process. Figure 5.14 shows us an example of the *Set a new user account* use case that is using the *Retrieve from employee records* use case to check that the user does not exist before adding the new record.

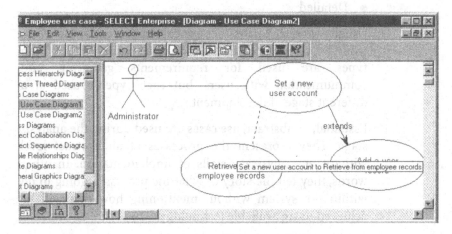

Figure 5.14 Adding a uses link.

Figure 5.15 shows us an example of the two distinctive links between use cases that are extends and uses.

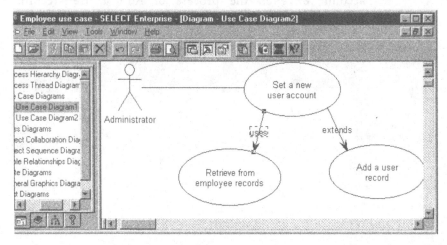

Figure 5.15 A use case linked to other use cases.

Abstract and detailed use cases

They are two main types of use cases:

- Abstract
- Detailed

Usually we refer to abstract use cases as essential use cases, while we refer to detailed use cases as real use cases. Both types are used for requirements gathering and communication with users, but each type is used at a different stage of development.

Essential, or abstract, use cases are used during the analysis stage. They represent the processes at an abstract level without any physical details of implementation. In other words, they tell the story of what the process is going to do within the system without mentioning how that will be achieved using available technology.

Real, or detailed, use cases extend the essential use cases during the design stage to tell the story of how the process will be carried out physically using existing technologies. This includes details of interfaces, steps of processing and so on. Sometimes diagrammatic use cases are accompanied by textual use cases at this stage.

Essential and real use cases will be discussed again in Chapter 11 when we move from analysis to design.

Requirements gathering and analysis

The first step of software development, especially in client-oriented systems, is requirements gathering. During requirements gathering, we try to identify the specifications of the system under development. These specifications should reflect the end-user requirements, which may be functional or non-functional. As an example of functional requirements, the user may request special printing facilities within the system. Non-functional requirements may be interface requirements or documentation requirements. The process of converting these requirements into specifications is referred to as requirements analysis or systems analysis.

In the past, analysts converted requirements into formal specifications, which are not always easy for the user to understand. Use cases provide us with a diagrammatic means of communicating with users during the process of gathering and analyzing requirements. We can utilize use cases as a powerful tool of communication with end users to ensure the correctness of analysis. It is easier for non-technical end users to understand diagrammatic rather than formal representation of process.

Chapter 6

Classes and Objects

Introduction

The underlying concepts of object-oriented analysis and design are class and object. Every class is defined in terms of data and operations, or methods, that are performed on that data. Class modelling describes a system's static structure in terms of classes, associations and characteristics of these classes (methods and attributes).

Objects are instances of classes. We can view the class as a general description of a set of objects. As an example, a description of a car provides a general description that applies to Ford Escort and BMW 3 Series cars, amongst others. The description of the car is the description of the class structure; Ford Escort and BMW 3 Series are instances of the *Car* class.

Associations are the links between classes, which underline the relationship, collaboration, and communication between the associated classes. There are several types of links that can be used to relate one class to another.

In this chapter we will look at:

- Classes and objects
- Class types
- Class structure
- Class diagrams
- Class links
- Abstract and detailed class diagrams.

Classes and objects

A class is a general description of a set of objects that share a common structure and a common behaviour. Classes are described in terms of attributes (data) and operations (or methods). The attributes of each object are declared in the class of which the object is an instantiation but take values specific to that object. Methods are defined once, in their class, but can be executed on any object that is a member of the class. An association between classes is an abstraction of the constituent links between objects.

The class diagram notation in SELECT Enterprise is based on UML. Complex class diagrams can be managed by using packages, which we cover in Chapter 12, to provide a containment mechanism for various classes within the model.

Class types

SELECT Enterprise distinguishes between business and user classes (see Figure 6.1).

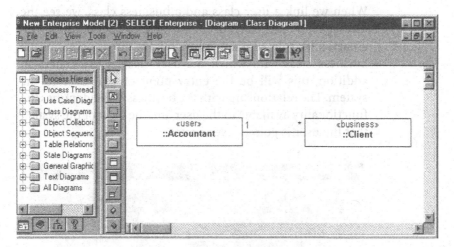

Figure 6.1 User and business classes.

User classes define the user interface, which we cover in Chapter 13. Business classes are the main classes that have the responsibility for carrying the functionality of the systems or sub-systems. Figure 6.2 shows an example of business classes and the relationships between them.

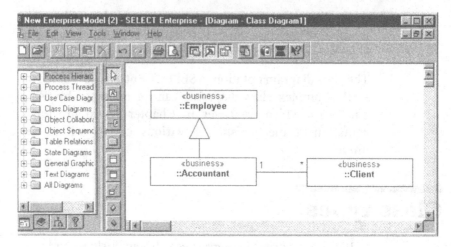

Figure 6.2 *Relationships between business classes.*

When we link a user class and a business class, we see the message in Figure 6.3. A user class defines a set of users with a particular role who are going to have direct access to the business class with which the user class is associated. In addition, this will be the entry point of that user to the system. The relationship with the business class identifies the functionality available to the user and the view of the system that the user is going to see or use.

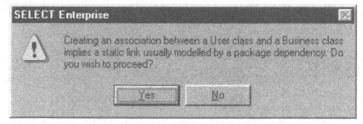

Figure 6.3 *An informative message about linking business and user classes.*

In addition to business and user classes, which are distinguished in SELECT Enterprise, there are other types of classes, which are usually used during the design phase. These classes appear as a result of resolving an association or dealing with data persistence.

- Collection classes are used to resolve many-to-many class associations. We will look at these classes briefly within this chapter when we discuss associations.
- Data management classes are used to manage data. These will be covered in more detail in Chapter 14 when we discuss databases.

SELECT Enterprise does not provide distinctive representations of these classes: business classes are used to represent them

Class structure

The class structure is based on two OO concepts: encapsulation and responsibility. Encapsulation means that all the information or data that define the class and all the methods that will be used with this data are - gathered together in one capsule, that is, the class itself. Responsibility, on the other hand, enables us to decide what goes into the class and what does not. Each class has a specified responsibility, which can be one or more of the following:

- Holding data (as for collection or data management classes)
- Providing a user interface
- Providing am interface to other modules within the system
- Providing business functionality (such as calculating the sub-totals in an invoice class)

To explain what we mean by class structure, let us assume that we are trying to build a program that maintains information about students' academic achievement. We will have a *Student* class, a *Module* class and an *Achievement* class.

Creating class diagrams

To create our first class diagram we can use the File | New Diagram | Class Diagram menu option, as shown in Figure 6.4.

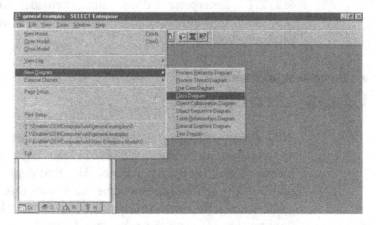

Figure 6.4 Creating a class diagram.

This will give us a clear screen (see Figure 6.5) to which we can add classes to build our class diagram.

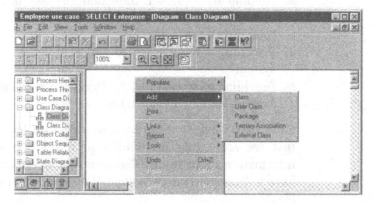

Figure 6.5 Adding a new class to a class diagram.

You may notice in Figure 6.5 that there are five possible elements that can be added to the class diagram:

- Class
- User class
- Package
- Ternary association
- External class

Our focus within this chapter is on business classes (created by the Class option). The result of selecting the Add | Class option can be seen in Figure 6.6.

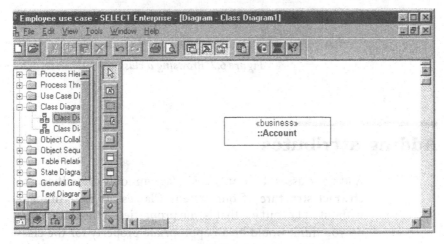

Figure 6.6 Newly added business class.

SELECT Enterprise gives us the facility to rename the class. I have changed the name of the class to *Account*.

Browsing a class

SELECT Enterprise contains the Browse Class utility, which you can find by clicking on a selected class (see Figure 6.7).

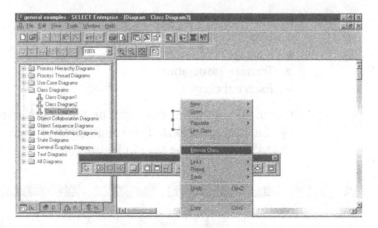

Figure 6.7 *Browsing a class.*

Adding attributes

Adding classes to our class diagram only identifies the abstract structure of our system. Classes are not complete without `attributes`, that is, the properties of the class. What do you think would be an appropriate property for the class *Account* from Figure 6.6? Figure 6.8 shows the class with the attribute *Account Number*. How did we add the attribute to the class? How do we identify the appropriate properties of a class?

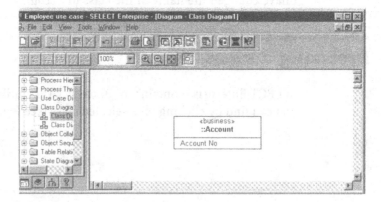

Figure 6.8 *The* Account *class with the* Account No *attribute.*

We have two ways to add an attribute, either by using the Attribute button on the class diagram toolbox (see Figure 6.9) or by browsing the class (see Figure 6.10).

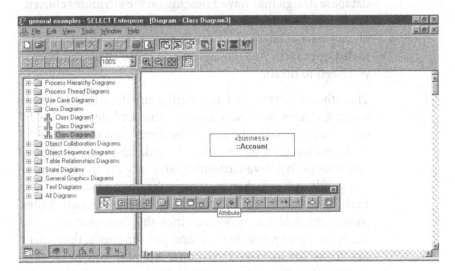

Figure 6.9 Adding an attribute using the class diagram toolbox.

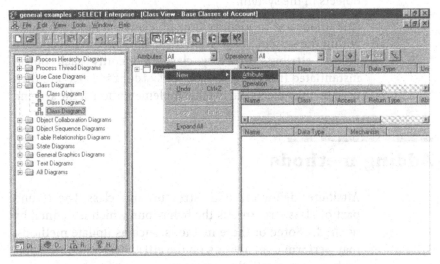

Figure 6.10 Adding an attribute using the Browse Class utility.

The question to answer now is how do we identify the properties of the class? It is very difficult to answer this question with a set of rules that can be followed in sequence. Experience plays a large part in deciding what class attributes should be included. Also the limitations of database design may have a bearing on the attributes chosen. Try to keep the class simple and focused on the requirements of that particular class as much as you can. Adapt a minimalist approach, you can always add more attributes later if you need to do so.

The other general rule I use during my design, is to think along the lines of class identity, name and description. In other words, what is the role of the given class in my design? As an example, let us assume we are developing a shopping cart system. We have customers who will use the system to buy goods. It is safe then to assume there is a *Customer* class. Each object of this class would have at least the attributes *Name* and *Address*. However, since the customer uses the shopping cart system to shop and pay for goods, then there has to be an invoice, a customer account and perhaps a history of previous transactions. Now we can see how the objects of the *Customer* class evolve in relation to other objects in the system.

It is important to identify how objects relate to each other within the system. It is a good idea, therefore, to introduce a unique attribute to every class to identify each object instantiated from the class. Object identifiers are then used to link objects during the implementation of the system.

Adding methods

Attributes define the static structure of a class. The second part of class structure is the behaviour, which is defined by methods. Some of these methods, such as update methods, may perform operations on the attributes; other methods, such as get methods, may provide interfaces with other objects; or they may perform a business operation such as calculating subtotals of some invoice. Figure 6.11 shows our *Account* class with the *Print Account Details* method added.

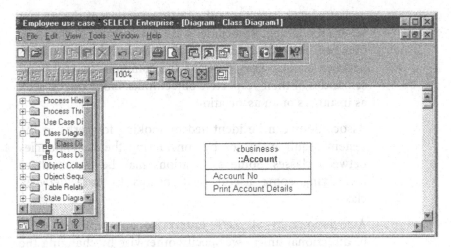

Figure 6.11 Print method added to the Account *class.*

To add a method you follow the same steps as for adding an attribute. You can do this through the `Browse Class` utility or by clicking on the `Operation` button on the toolbox (next to the `Attribute` button). The difficulty is to identify which methods are required. It is impossible to give definitive rules that you can follow. One of the rules I usually use, however, is what may be called the *method-attribute-reliance* rule. The basic idea behind this rule is that all attributes in a class are private to the class and hence their values are private to their respective objects. Therefore, if there are any attributes to be accessed by other objects of any given class there should be a method that allows such access. This even applies between objects of the same class. As a result I would add methods such as *Set*, *Get*, and *Print* to all the classes that have attributes to be changed and that are responsible for maintaining data.

Class links

Class links represent physical or conceptual connections between classes or objects, often referred to as `associations`. Associations between classes, together with class methods and attributes, constitute the static structure of the system we are modelling. Associations are abstractions of the links between objects, representing the structural relationships between classes. They describe the common structure and semantics of their respective object links. Links can be seen as instances of an association.

Associations can be identified by looking for verbs in the system requirements or by considering the dependencies between classes. Some associations may be the result of identifying some useful relationships to have between classes.

Associations in SELECT Enterprise are represented as bi-directional unless we specify otherwise by changing the arrows representing the directed association from the properties window. It is good practice to name associations descriptively. In SELECT Enterprise, each end of an association is referred to as a role. In addition, we can add constraints to the description of the associations. Constraints are functional relationships between objects that restrict the range of values which can be assumed by interacting objects.

Many-to-many associations should be resolved as part of moving from the analysis phase to the design phase. A new collection or link class may be created to resolve a many-to-many relationship. A collection class contains attributes identifying the objects that are linked by it. Some methods are usually added in addition to the attributes. For example, _First_, _Last_ and _Next_ methods are typical methods of collection classes.

Inheritance

Inheritance is a key concept of object-oriented analysis and design. It allows classes to share their characteristics within a hierarchy and yet preserve their differences. Note that inheritance works at the class level and not at the object level. The introduction of inheritance into a model can be done in several ways. However you should use inheritance sparingly, as you will see later.

The introduction of inheritance associations between classes leads to the formation of a tree structure in which there is a super-class linked to its subclasses. Each subclass inherits the characteristics of its associated super-class.

Another way to look at inheritance is in the reverse direction from subclass to super-class. We can say that a super-class is the generalization of its subclasses. Consequently, we can say that subclasses are specializations of the super-class.

Inheritance allows us to abstract behaviour (methods) and characteristics (attributes) that are common to different classes into a common super-class. If this super-class has no direct instances we would usually call it an abstract super-class. However its behaviour and properties are inherited by all instances of its subclasses.

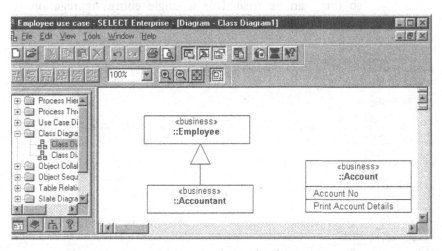

Figure 6.12 An inheritance relationship between two classes.

Inheritance is represented on a class diagram by an unfilled triangle that points up to the super-class (see Figure 6.12). Inheritance modelling in SELECT Enterprise is referred to in terms of generalization and specialization. A class can inherit features from more than one super-class, called multiple inheritance. However, this may lead to unnecessary complexity in design and difficulty in maintenance, and should be avoided where possible.

Inheritance is the facilitator of reusability. At the same time inheritance has a strong impact on the robustness of design. Therefore, inheritance has to be used with care. It can have a negative impact in terms of introducing new classes or modifying methods on classes in the inheritance line.

Aggregation and composition

Aggregation is a special form of association in which aggregates are made up of objects from different classes. An aggregation indicates that the objects of which the aggregation is composed are part-of the aggregate object. The benefits of aggregation are that it allows different objects to be linked so they can be treated as a single entity. Aggregation is represented by a diamond touching an object (see Figure 6.13).

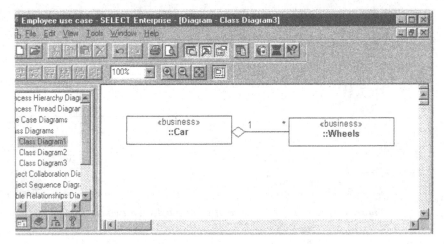

Figure 6.13 *An aggregation relationship between two classes.*

Composition is a special case of aggregation with extra restrictions. In composition, the whole-part relationship between the aggregate and the aggregated objects is stronger than in an aggregation relationship. This means that if the main object, in other words the aggregate object, ceases to exist or is affected by an operation, such as copying, all the parts of this object are affected. In other words, all the objects that participate in the composition relationship are affected by what happens to the aggregate object. Composition is represented in UML in a similar way to aggregation but with a filled diamond. This is not available in SELECT Enterprise. However we can have the same effect by using constraints over the relationship to indicate composition.

Adding inheritance

To identify inheritance relationships between classes, we need to identify classes that can be seen as a type-of or a type-for in relation to other classes. A type-of relationship identifies sub-classes, whereas a type-for identifies super-classes.

It is clear that there may be several types of employee, such as managers, directors, clerks and accountants, in the company. We may need different attributes or methods for each of these classes of employees. Figure 6.12 shows an example of an inheritance relationship between *Accountant* and *Employee*.

To add an inheritance relationship between two classes, we can use the `Inheritance` button on the toolbox.

Adding relationships

Relationships, or associations, between classes are very similar to the relationships we may see in entity relationship diagrams in database design. Figure 6.14 shows the adding of a relationship between two classes. We can find these relationships on the toolbox bar.

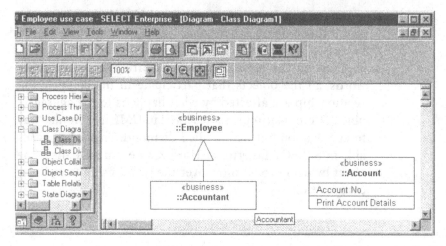

Figure 6.14 Adding a relationship using the toolbox.

Figure 6.15 shows a one-to-many relationship between two classes.

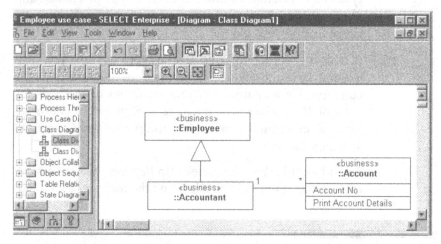

Figure 6.15 A one-to-many relationship between two classes.

In UML, we can create many-to-many relationships, which then have to be resolved during design in a similar manner to resolving many-to-many relationships in a relational database. However, SELECT Enterprise does not support many-to-many relationships. This forces us to think about resolving such relationships at an early stage. The benefit of doing so is to prevent us from making wrong assumptions during analysis that cannot be supported during design. This also enforces the idea that analysis and design in OO methodologies are not distinctively separate as is the case with traditional methodologies.

In addition to relational database relationships, the research into software reuse and modern software engineering has produced relationships that relate to the grouping of several classes to form a bigger entity. In UML, there are two such associations: `aggregation` and `composition`. SELECT Enterprise, however, only supports aggregation.

Figure 6.13 shows an aggregation association between *Car* and *Wheels*. It is clear that a car is aggregated of several components such as wheels; however the destruction of a car does not lead necessarily to the destruction of its wheels. As a result, if we delete a *Car* object in a car design system, it does not necessary lead to the destruction of the *Wheels* objects related to the car. Figure 6.16 shows the aggregation relationship being added using the toolbox.

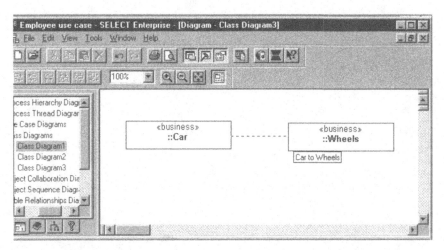

Figure 6.16 Adding an aggregation relationship using the toolbox.

Abstract and detailed class diagrams

The class diagram is central to OO analysis and design. Class diagrams are used during all the stages of OO analysis and design. We usually start with an abstract diagram in which only classes and perhaps some attributes and methods are identified. Other types of classes appear usually in the design class diagram (see Chapter 11).

Chapter

7

Modelling Interaction

Introduction

Object interaction modelling demonstrates the dynamic behaviour that occurs between objects by integrating the static class diagrams with the use cases.

The class diagram defines the internal structure of the classes but says nothing about how they inter-relate whereas use cases depict the operations between classes in the problem domain without reference to the internal structure of the classes themselves. In this chapter, we focus on how the objects interact reflecting their internal design and their function within use cases. In this chapter we will look at:

- Modelling class interactions
- Collaboration diagrams
- Sequence diagrams

Modelling class interactions

In earlier chapters, we have developed use cases and class diagrams. The use cases and class diagrams need to be crosschecked with each other and with the user requirements. This process of integrating use cases and class diagrams is an iterative process during which the users' view (the use case model) and the developers' view (the class model) is compared with the initial requirements and is refined.

Class interaction in UML is modelled using two types of modelling diagrams. These diagrams can also be used to model object interaction during the design phase when a detailed account of an interaction may be needed. Some documentation refers to them as class interaction diagrams but they may also be referred to as object interaction diagrams, which emphasises that they are used as part of the design process and that we may refer to particular objects of classes, which enables us to highlight interactions between individual objects including objects of the same class. These models are:

- The Class Sequence Diagram (CSD), which is used to describe a use case or an operation in terms of a time sequence which is represented implicitly by arrows running downwards.
- The Class Collaboration Diagram (CCD), which is used to describe a scenario of flow of messages between classes within a use case in a static time frame.

The diagrams are equivalent to each other. However Sequence Diagrams are more commonly used than Collaboration Diagrams when we want to emphasize the time factor of the interaction. Before we look at the actual construction of the diagrams, we need to look at two aspects of class interaction: delegation and the time factor.

Delegation

Delegation is the concept of passing responsibilities from one class to another. A minimalist approach is often followed in OO systems. Minimalism means each class should have clear and precise functions to perform within the system being developed. This function is the justification for the existence of such a class within the system. For example, a *Student* class has nothing to do with the function *Set a timetable*, therefore it should contain no function and hold no information about setting timetables. Too many classes increase system complexity and slow both its performance and development. The best guide in this is the object-oriented principle of encapsulation. In other words, each class has to contain all the attributes and methods that characterize the objects of the class decisively and distinctively and which provide the class with its uniqueness.

The responsibility of each class may be informative or functional, or both. As the responsibility of each class is defined decisively and individually, each class needs to interact with other classes in order to perform complex tasks collectively. This interaction is the basis of delegation. The importance of delegation and distribution of tasks and responsibilities become more apparent in networks and distributed systems such as Internet databases.

Time factor

Time is an important aspect that should be considered carefully during software development. Time becomes an even more critical factor in real-time, online and concurrent systems. In class diagrams there is no way of representing time and its impact on interaction between different classes and objects.

The time factor is represented during the development of sequence diagrams. The importance of including timing aspects is reflected by efforts being made in the recent development of real-time UML to serve the needs of real-time system designers.

Collaboration diagrams

We may use a class collaboration diagram (CCD) to illustrate the interactions between actors and classes or instances of the classes. A CCD is associated with use cases. Each CCD represents the interaction between classes or objects within the use case. While you may have one CCD for each use case, it is possible to have multiple CCDs for a single use case.

The one benefit of the CCD over the class sequence diagram (CSD) is that the CCD provides a visual representation of the structure of class collaborations which helps in identifying design patterns. In addition, the CCD enables us to experiment with alternative design structures with different objects as collaborators and controllers, which may also have different messages passing between them.

Creating a collaboration diagram

Creating a collaboration diagram, similar to the one presented in Figure 7.1, is similar to creating a class diagram or a use case diagram. In fact, you can use the existing classes and use cases to build your collaboration diagram. This is advisable since it maintains consistency between the collaboration diagram and the use case we are exploring.

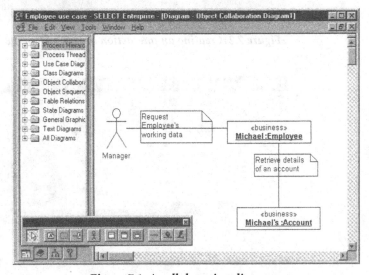

Figure 7.1 *A collaboration diagram.*

In Figure 7.1, you can identify some basic elements of a collaboration diagram. We have retained the actor from the use case we are exploring and the classes are related to the use case.

We can create a collaboration diagram in several ways. We can select the File | New Diagram | Object Collaboration Diagram menu option (Figure 7.2) or use the drop down menu (Figure 7.3).

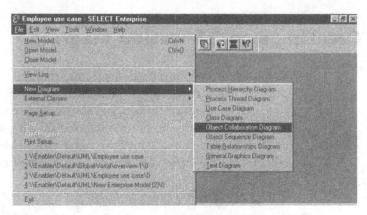

Figure 7.2 Creating an interaction diagram from the File menu.

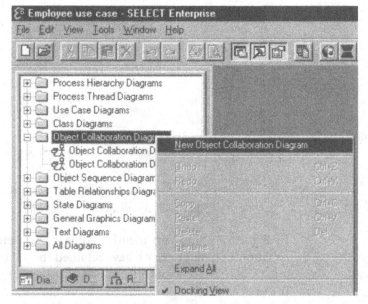

Figure 7.3 Creating an interaction diagram using
the right mouse button.

Another way is to create a child diagram from the use case we
are exploring (Figure 7.4).

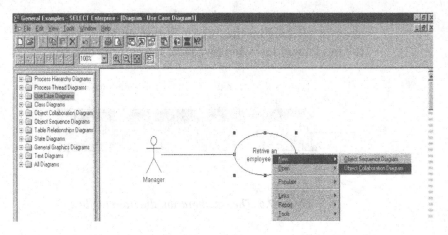

Figure 7.4 Creating an interaction diagram from a use case.

Once you have opened a new collaboration diagram, the best way to proceed is to insert the actors that we have already identified in the use case. That is straightforward: all you need to do is to right-click and select Add, as shown in Figure 7.5

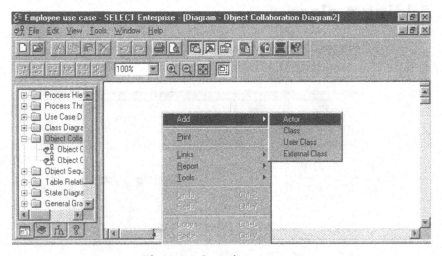

Figure 7.5 Inserting an actor.

Alternatively we can use the toolbox (Figure 7.6) to create an actor by clicking on the Actor button and then clicking on the model window where we want the actor to appear.

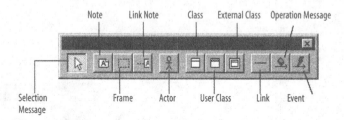

Figure 7.6 *The collaboration diagram toolbox.*

Once we have added the actor, it is time to add the main components of collaboration diagrams: classes and messages. It is important for us to decide whether we are using objects in the collaboration diagram or just classes. Also, now is the time to decide on the structure of the system, including the control pattern (that is, which class is a controller that sends messages between other classes).

Adding a class

Figure 7.7 shows the adding of a class to the diagram.

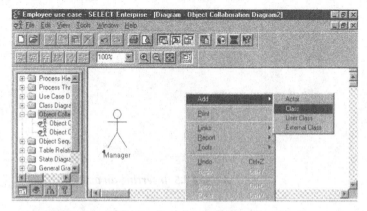

Figure 7.7 *Adding a class to a collaboration diagram.*

It is very likely that we will find the class we need to add in the list of existing classes that appears once we have chosen to add a class (Figure 7.8).

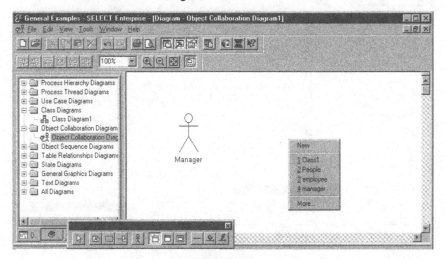

Figure 7.8 Adding existing or new classes.

However, we may discover the need for a new class we did not think about during the construction of the class diagram. We can add a new class to the collaboration diagram by selecting New from the drop down menu. Once we do so, the new class will be added to the data dictionary of the model and will be visible for use in other models. However, SELECT Enterprise will not update the class diagrams automatically, so we need to add the new class to the correct class diagram and update any links between that class and other classes.

Deleting a class

We have to be careful in deleting classes from a collaboration diagram (just as in other diagrams). If we want to remove a class from a collaboration diagram without removing it from the model, we click on the class and then either:

- Press the Delete key on the keyboard, or
- Select the Edit | Delete menu option, or
- Right-click and select Delete.

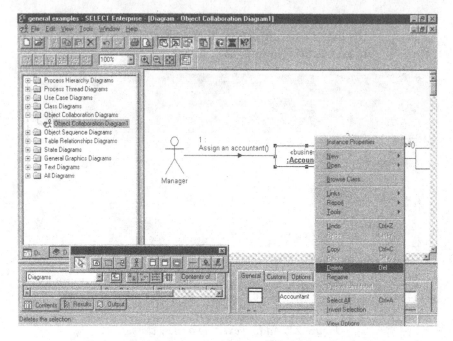

Figure 7.9 Deleting a class for a collaboration diagram.

This will not delete the class from the model, which means that the class still exists in the model dictionary and is still visible for use in other models. If our aim is to delete the class from the model, then we have to delete the class from the class diagram.

Editing relationships

The last step in creating a collaboration diagram is to add relationships and messages that reflect the relationships each class has with other classes in the class diagram. We can add events or operations to the relationships to specify their meanings within the collaboration diagram. Figure 7.10 shows a relationship with an operation. Note that we used the toolbox bar to add the operation on the relationship.

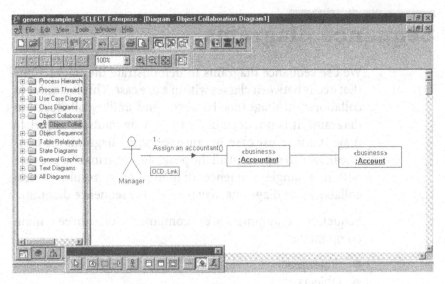

Figure 7.10 Adding an operation.

Figure 7.11 shows the second relationship with an event.

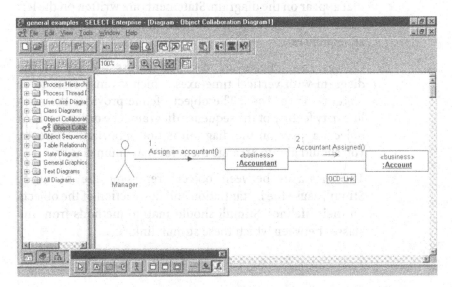

Figure 7.11 Adding an event.

Sequence diagrams

We use sequence diagrams to demonstrate the interactions that occur between classes within a use case. This is similar to collaboration diagrams. However, and unlike collaboration diagrams, it is not customary to provide multiple sequence diagrams for a use case. Because sequence diagrams are non-linear, we can represent all the possible scenarios of a use case within a single sequence diagram. As a result, several collaboration diagrams may map to one sequence diagram.

Sequence diagrams are composed of three main components:

- Statements
- Objects
- Stimuli

A `statement` describes in structured English the processes that appear on the diagram. Statements are written on the left hand side of the diagram. We sometimes refer to statements as sequences.

Classes and objects are declared across the top of the diagram with vertical time-axes, which we may refer to as `object lifelines`. The object lifeline provides the non-linearity feature of the sequence diagram. The order in which objects appear on the diagram is not important. However, you should aim to arrange them for maximum clarity.

The messages between objects represent the `stimuli`. Stimuli cause the instantiation and destruction of the objects on their lifelines. Stimuli should map to methods from the classes between which these stimuli link.

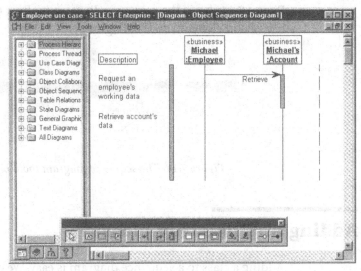

Figure 7.12 A sequence diagram.

Creating a sequence diagram

Figure 7.13 shows that we can start a new sequence diagram using the right mouse button.

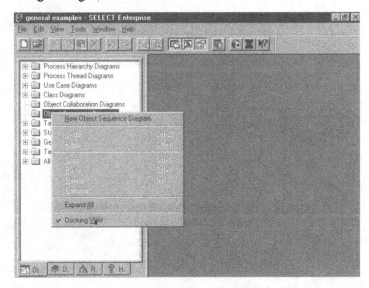

Figure 7.13 Creating a new sequence diagram.

Figure 7.14 shows the sequence diagram toolbox that we can use to add elements to the diagram.

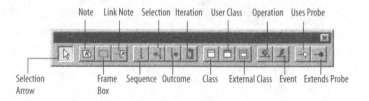

Note   Link Note   Selection   Iteration   User Class   Operation   Uses Probe

Selection   Frame   Sequence   Outcome   Class   External Class   Event   Extends Probe
Arrow   Box

Figure 7.14 The sequence diagram toolbox.

Adding and deleting classes

Adding a class to a sequence diagram is easy. We click on the `Class` button in the toolbox and then click on the place in the diagram that we want the class to appear.

If we want to add an existing class to the diagram, it is easier to do so by right-clicking on the diagram and selecting the `Class` option. Figure 7.15 shows that we then see a drop down list of existing classes.

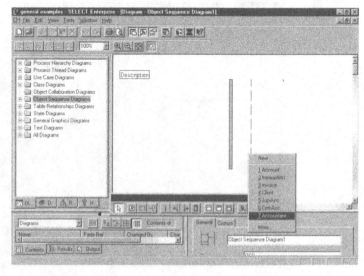

Figure 7.15 The Enabler administration tool.

When the class appears on the diagram we may choose to define an instance of the class. This allows us to show the interaction between objects as well. If we are not interested in this level of detail we can leave the word Instance before the class name to refer to any instance of the class, or just keep the class name to mean that this interaction applies to all the class members. We must always remember that adding a class to the sequence diagram is related to the use case that this sequence diagram represents.

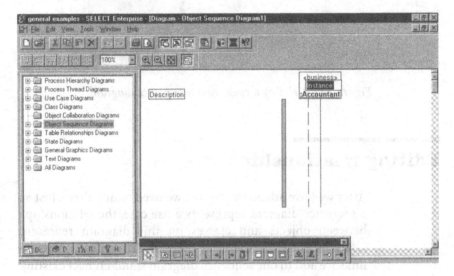

Figure 7.16 *A class and its lifeline.*

The facility for deleting classes from a sequence diagram is limited. We cannot delete the class from the model; we can only delete it from the diagram on which we are working (Figure 7.17). This is designed to maintain the consistency between diagrams within the model. If we need to delete a class completely from the model we have to do so from the class diagram.

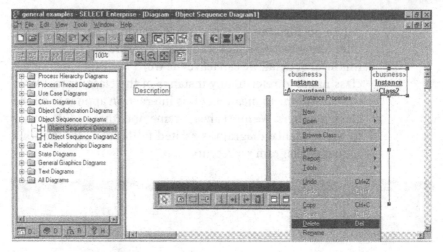

Figure 7.17 Deleting a class from a sequence diagram.

Editing relationships

After we have added the classes we need to link them. Just as a sequence diagram represents a use case, the relationships between objects and classes on this diagram represent relationships from the class diagram. This means that the links we add to our sequence diagram should reflect existing relationships or associations between classes. As a result we have a vertical dimension (use case processes) and a horizontal dimension (class diagram relationships and methods) to consider.

There are three types of sequence that can be added to describe links between classes in a sequence diagram, which are often referred to as transactional links:

- Sequence
- Iteration
- Selection

Figure 7.18 shows these types of links between classes.

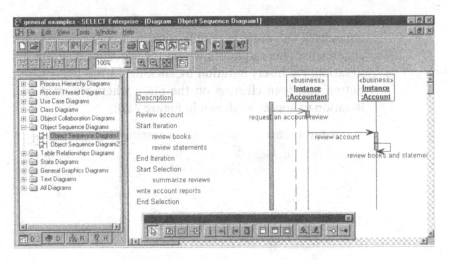

Figure 7.18 Sequences between classes.

Adding a sequence description

Let us take, as an example, an account review process. The sequence diagram may start with a general Review account step, which is inserted using the Sequence button on the toolbox as shown in Figure 7.19.

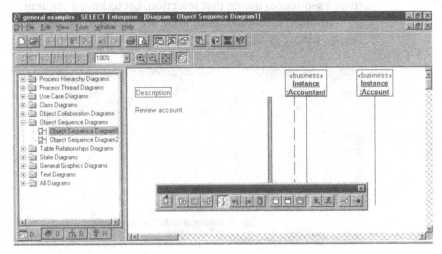

Figure 7.19 Adding a sequence.

Once the account is reviewed, the second step is to review and crosscheck the account details such as account books and statements. This can be shown on the sequence diagram by iteration. We insert iteration by clicking on the `Iteration` button and then clicking on the place where we want the iteration to appear as shown in Figure 7.20.

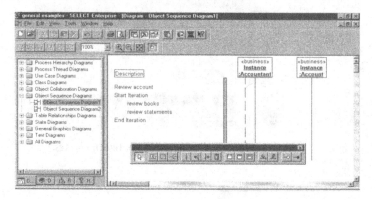

Figure 7.20 Adding an iteration.

The outcome of the review could be in the form of a report. You may notice that you cannot add an outcome unless you add a selection first. So let us add a selection using the `Selection` button from the toolbox. A selection sequence is a structured sequence similar to iteration. Therefore we need to add sequences inside that selection. Let us have a sequence of Summarize reviews and then an outcome of account review report as shown in Figure 7.21.

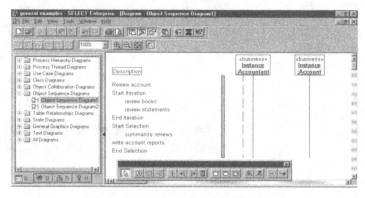

Figure 7.21 Creating a new datastore.

Now we have our process outlined in sequential statements, but nothing shows the interaction between classes during the statements.

Adding interaction between classes

As we have seen, sequences are textual descriptions of what is happening in the sequence diagram. The next step of building a sequence diagram is to visualise the class interaction through adding diagrammatic links. These links include events and operations.

An event is an external stimulus. It is very likely to be a user or external process intervention. Modern programming languages, such as Visual Basic and Java, provide event-based programming capabilities and in many cases professional programming in these languages relies heavily on those capabilities. In our example, let us assume that the user requested an account review. There is an event, which causes the *Accountant* class to respond as shown in Figure 7.22.

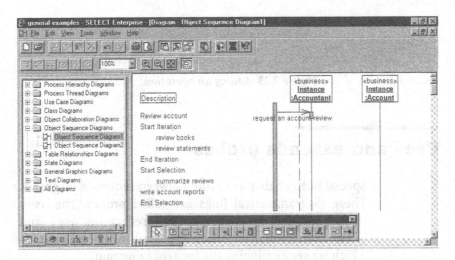

Figure 7.22 Adding an event.

Note that the *Accountant* class is a business class, while the event is coming from a user. This is a strong indication that we will need an interface class to receive this event and initiate the *Accountant* object.

An operation, unlike an event, is part of the class. Operations represent methods within the targeted class. So let us assume that the *Accountant* object requests the account review from the *Account* object. Let us also assume that the account review triggers an internal operation within the *Account* to review statements and books. Both *review account* and *review books and statements,* which are shown in Figure 7.23, are methods within the *Account* class.

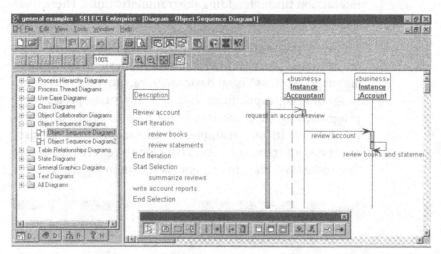

Figure 7.23 Adding an operation.

Uses and extends probes

Special links enable us to link between sequence diagrams. These diagrammatical links are called probes. The uses probe and the extends probe reflect the uses and extends links that may have appeared in the use case for which we are developing the sequence diagram.

Modelling
Behaviour

Introduction

It is important to identify how classes behave over time. This is often called dynamic modelling and reflects the temporal aspects of a system. In this chapter we will look at:

- Dynamic modelling
- State diagrams
- State messages
- Super and sub-states
- Activity diagrams

Dynamic modelling

The dynamic model describes the system aspects that are concerned with time and the sequencing of operations. These operations can be events that mark changes, sequences of events, and the organization of events and states. The dynamic model is not, however, concerned with what the operations do or how they are implemented.

The dynamic model is represented graphically by a set of state diagrams. Each state diagram models all the possible states of a class and the event sequences permitted for that class in response to external events. A state diagram can be seen as a behavioural template for the class it is modelling. A state diagram shows the states and the transitions between those states through which an object passes during its lifetime, together with its responses to external stimuli. We usually create state diagrams for classes whose objects have a definite life cycle or exhibit significant behaviour.

State diagrams allow us to check the consistency of the functionality and relationships of classes. Thus they are often compared with class diagrams to check structural correctness in response to the functional requirements of the classes under scrutiny.

State diagrams

A state diagram describes the behaviour of a class. In SELECT Enterprise, a state diagram may also describe the behaviour of an operation. Figure 8.1 shows an example of a full state diagram. Notice the start and result states, which identify the beginning and end of the state diagram.

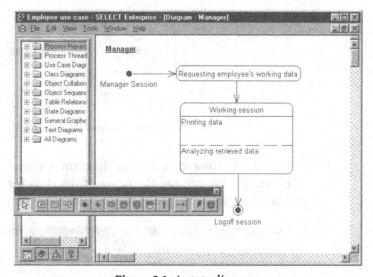

Figure 8.1 A state diagram.

State diagrams can model:

- States and operations within these states
- Events that trigger operations or lead to new states
- Transitions between states
- Super and sub-states.

Creating a state diagram

As mentioned earlier a state diagram describes the behaviour of a class or an operation. As a result, it must always be created as a child diagram of a class or operation as shown in

Figure 8.2. State diagrams cannot be created as unattached diagrams.

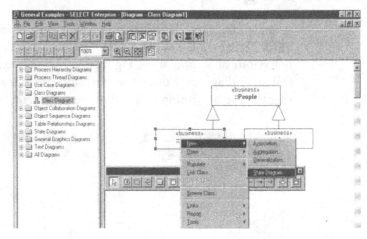

Figure 8.2 Creating a new state diagram.

Figure 8.3 shows the new state diagram that was initiated in Figure 8.2. We can see the name of the class for which this state diagram is created at the top of the diagram.

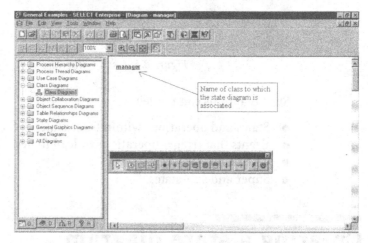

Figure 8.3 A new state diagram for the manager class.

Figure 8.4 shows the state diagram toolbox bar, which enables you to edit state diagrams easily.

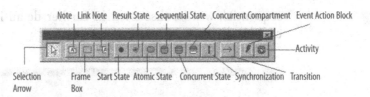

Figure 8.4 A new state diagram for the manager class.

States

The state diagram is formed of a sequence of states. Each state represents a condition or situation of an object at some point from the object's creation to its destruction. The object stays in the same state until some external stimulus triggers a change that leads to a new state. We will look at external stimuli and transitions from one state to another later in this chapter. A state can be one of the following:

- A start state, which indicates the point of object initiation. A class can have multiple initial states depending on the events causing object instantiation.
- A result state, which indicates that an object ceases to exist. A class can have multiple result states associated with different events that lead to object destruction.
- Sequential or concurrent states, which are complex states that consist of several atomic states. Sequential and concurrent states are often referred to as super-states.
- An atomic state, which is a normal simple state that represents an object between start and result states. An atomic state can be added as a sub-state to sequential and concurrent states.

Adding and deleting states

Figure 8.5 shows the addition of a state by right-clicking on the diagram. Note that the states you can add are listed in the menu. Some of these states, such as concurrent and sequential, will be discussed in further detail later in this chapter.

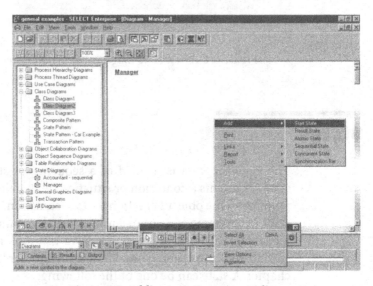

Figure 8.5 Adding a state to a state diagram.

A state can be deleted by selecting that option from the drop down menu as shown in Figure 8.6. Note that if we delete the state from the model, it will be completely removed and will not be available for other state diagrams.

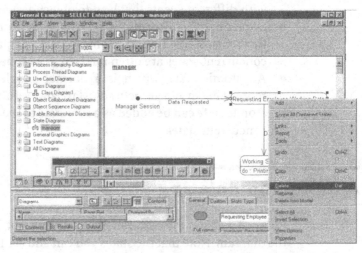

Figure 8.6 Deleting a state from a state diagram.

Editing states

There are two main components of an atomic state: events and operations. Figure 8.7 shows an event block added to a state using the toolbox bar.

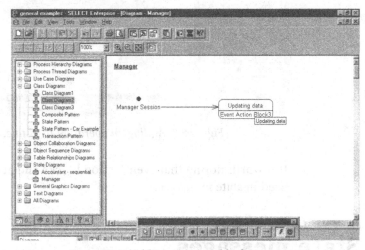

Figure 8.7 Adding an event block to a state.

An event usually refers to stimuli that may occur while the object resides in a particular state, which leads to an action but does not necessarily change the state of the object. As an example, the event may be a request for information from another object without changing the values or status of any of the object's attributes. Thus the object remains in the same state.

Operations are added to atomic states to show that the object is doing something while it resides in that state. Operations are represented as activities. Figure 8.8 shows an atomic state with an operation.

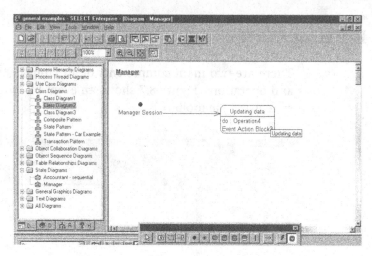

Figure 8.8 Adding an operation to a state.

It is worth noting that event/action blocks and activities are used in state messages.

State messages

Some state messages indicate state changes. In other words, they describe events that cause the object to move from its current state to a new state. Some state messages communicate with other objects. These include the actions that the given object may perform which may lead to change in the states of other objects.

In this section we will look at the building blocks of state messages. These blocks are formed from the basic elements of event and action, and the complex structures of transaction and action blocks. We should always remember that the more complex structures are built from the basic elements, which means that they are not much more complicated to deal with than the elementary events and actions. We will look first at the basic elements of `event`, `action`, `activity` **and** `condition`.

Events

An event describes some external stimulus to an object that denotes in which circumstances the object under scrutiny will move to a new state. This may happen as a result of some action that is triggered by the event. An event is represented in state diagram by an event/action block. Figure 8.9 shows a start state and an atomic state linked by an event.

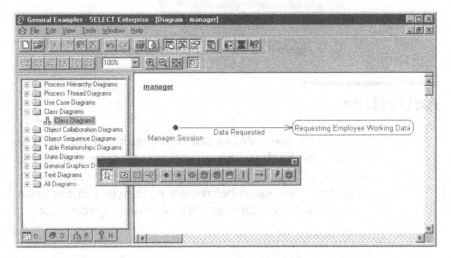

Figure 8.9 An event triggered by a user action.

Actions

An action is a functional response to an event. It is an optional part of the event/action block, which we will see later on as a complex structure built from events and actions. We can also use actions as part of a transition between two states or within a state. When we use actions on a transition we use the following UML notation:

```
<EventName>/<ActionName>
```

Figure 8.10 shows an example of two states linked with an event/action transition.

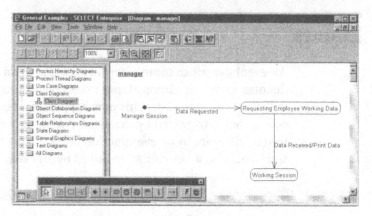

Figure 8.10 *An action in response to an event.*

Activities

We use activities within a state to represent an operation or method in the class. This operation is performed when the class is in the given state. In other words, we use activities to represent continuous behaviours of the class in the given state. We use the following UML notation to specify this:

```
do: <ActivityName>
```

In Figure 8.11 we can see an example of activity within a state.

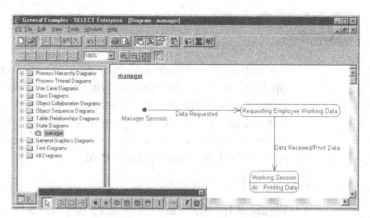

Figure 8.11 *An activity within a state.*

Conditions

We use conditions to control the triggering of transitions. They are very much like if-then statements in programming. The transition we are guarding with a condition will happen only when the condition is true. If we do not include an event in the transition description, the transition will happen as soon as the guarding condition is satisfied. We use the following UML notation, including the brackets, to describe conditions on the state diagram:

```
[<VariableName> <= <Condition>].
```

Figure 8.12 shows a transition between two states that is guarded by a condition.

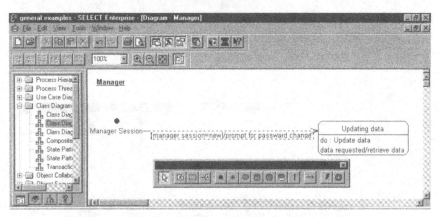

Figure 8.12 A condition guarding a transition.

Transitions

A transition consists of events, conditions, actions and activities. Transitions represent the reasons for change within the model, which lead the program or class to change its state. Therefore transitions appear between states on the state diagram, usually in the form of an event/action block.

Transitions may, for example, be caused by the execution of a method within the class or the calling of a method from external classes.

Adding and deleting transitions

We can add a transition to the state diagram using the toolbox. Click on the `Transition` button, the state from which the transition is to start and finally on the state to which the transition is directed. Alternatively, as shown in Figure 8.13, we can click on the state from which the transition starts and right-click to select the `Transition` option.

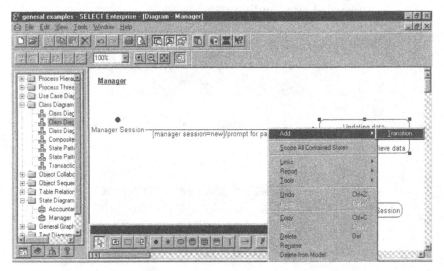

Figure 8.13 Adding a transition to a state diagram.

To delete a transition, select it and then right-click. We can then delete the transition from the diagram (using the `Delete` option) or from the model, which means that the transition will not be available for other state diagrams. Figure 8.14 shows the deletion of a transition from the model.

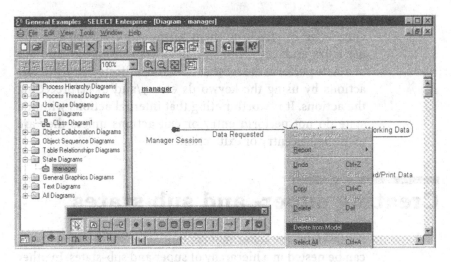

Figure 8.14 Deleting a transition from the model.

Editing transitions

Editing a transition is very similar to editing a state. We can add event/action blocks and activities to transitions. The meaning of event/action blocks and activities are the same as for states. The difference is that the events or activities affect the state of the object and the object moves from one state to another.

We add event/action blocks or activities by clicking on their respective buttons on the toolbox and then clicking on the transition we want to edit. Alternatively, we can click on the transition, right-click and select the option we require.

Event/action blocks

We use event/action blocks to model optional actions and activities. We can use event/action blocks within states or attach them to transitions. We can include events, actions, activities and conditions in event/action blocks.

You can define entry and exit actions on states as an alternative to attaching them to transitions. Typically, you use entry and exit actions when all transitions into and out of a state perform the same action. You indicate entry and exit actions by using the keywords entry/and exit/preceding the actions. It is worth noting that internal actions within a state do not perform entry or exit actions unless they are identified as entry or exit actions.

Creating super- and sub-states

Super-states are states that contain other states. Super-states can be nested in a hierarchy of super and sub-states. In other words, a sub-state may contain further sub-states until we reach an atomic state. Figure 8.15 shows an example of a super-state with two atomic sub-states.

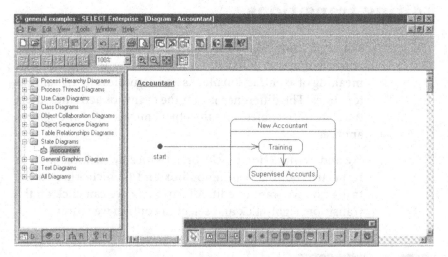

Figure 8.15 A super-state with two sub-states.

Super-states simplify the complexity of state diagrams by using generalization and aggregation concepts. The sub-states inherit from the super-state all the state activities and event/action blocks. In UML, there are two types of super-state (see Figures 8.16 and 8.17).

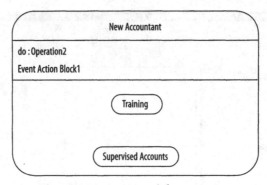

Figure 8.16 A sequential super-state.

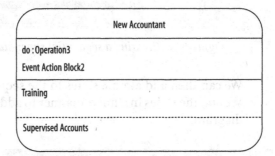

Figure 8.17 A concurrent super-state.

These two types are discussed next.

Sequential States

A sequential state is a super-state that holds sequential sub-
states and nested sub-states. For example, consider a
personnel software system in an accounting firm. Let us
assume that, when this accounting firm hires a new
accountant, the accountant has some in-house training and
then looks after some accounts under supervision. When
the accountant completes this program, a new state is
achieved. We can model that (see Figure 8.18) by starting
with a sequential super-state using the Sequential state
button.

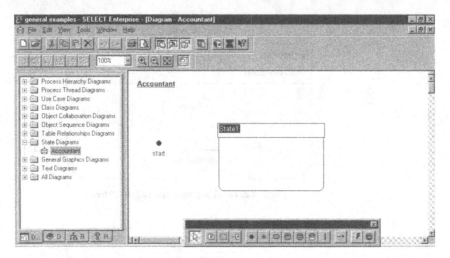

Figure 8.18 Creating a sequential super-state.

We can then add atomic states to the sequential super-state. We add the states in similar manner to adding states to a state diagram.

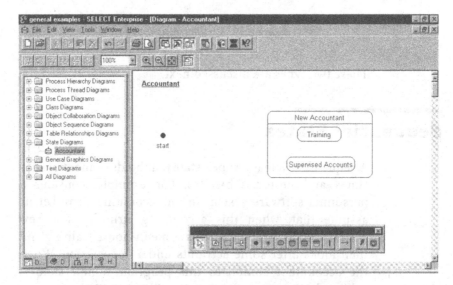

Figure 8.19 Creating sub-states within the super-state.

Figure 8.19 shows that we have added the two sub-states of *Training* and *Supervised Accounts*. These are the sub-states through which the new accountant needs to move before being fully qualified to work independently within the firm. Now we can add the transitions to produce the diagram in Figure 8.20.

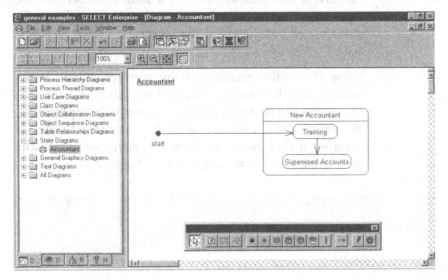

Figure 8.20 An example of a sequential super-state.

If we add any operations or event/action blocks to the super-state, they will apply to all sub-states. We can exit the super-state from any of the sub-states. In some cases, we may need to do so to show different possible exits. The exit transition from the super-state usually links the final state in the sequence to the next atomic or super-state unless there are several possible exits. If there are several exits, we would have several transitions linking one or more sub-states to the states that follow the sequential super-state.

Concurrent States

A concurrent state is a super-state that contains two or more sub-states that exist in parallel. An object that has concurrent states performs the associated activities concurrently. The sub-states are not synchronized. As with sequential states, concurrent states may have one or more exits, however each sub-state must be completed before the object can move out of the super-state. The control mechanism is split between concurrent activities, as shown by a dashed line between the sub-states. The control is then merged again when these sub-states are all complete and the object has moved to a new state.

Using the earlier example of the new accountant, let us assume that the firm has changed its policy and the new accountant can manage supervised accounts during training. In this case, the new accountant has concurrent states of *Training* and *Supervised Accounts*. First, we insert the concurrent state in our diagram, as in Figure 8.21.

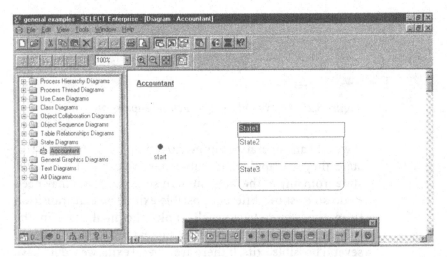

Figure 8.21 Creating a concurrent super-state.

Note the sub-states are added when we insert the concurrent state, with a dashed line separating them. We change the names of the sub-states.

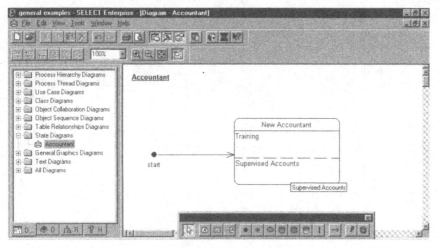

Figure 8.22 An example of a concurrent super-state.

We have to take extra care when we have more than one possible exit from the super-state. We usually represent this by using a separate transition for each sub-state. On the completion of a sub-state, the transition emerging from that sub-state will terminate the concurrency without waiting for the other sub-states to complete.

Activity diagrams

We can look at activity diagrams as a type of state diagram. The difference between activity diagrams and state diagrams is that activity diagrams show the activities and their dependencies. SELECT does not provide separate support for activity diagrams, however we can use the tools available for state diagrams to draw an activity diagram. Alternatively, we can draw activity diagrams as General Graphics Diagrams.

Chapter 9

SELECT Enterprise Extras

Introduction

SELECT Enterprise provides numerous extra tools that allow more flexibility in developing the models and converting them into code. These extra tools are not part of UML, however it is useful to know about them to benefit from the full potential of SELECT Enterprise. In this chapter we will look at:

- General graphics diagrams
- The Storage Mapper
- The data dictionary
- Checking the consistency of our models
- Code generators.

General graphics

In addition to the specific UML diagrams provided, we can use SELECT Enterprise General Graphics Diagrams to develop types of diagram that are not otherwise supported by either SELECT Enterprise or UML. For example, data flow charts are not supported, however for programmers with a background in structured methods, data flow charts are a useful tool for following the flow of programs and algorithms.

General graphics diagrams consist of shapes, known as nodes, and connections, known as flows, which link between the nodes. We can also link flows to dictionary items.

Storage Mapper

Once we have generated our business analysis models it is useful to generate the matching database structure to store data. In SELECT Enterprise, we use the Storage Mapper, which is shown in Figure 9.1, to do so automatically. We open the Storage Mapper from the Tools menu.

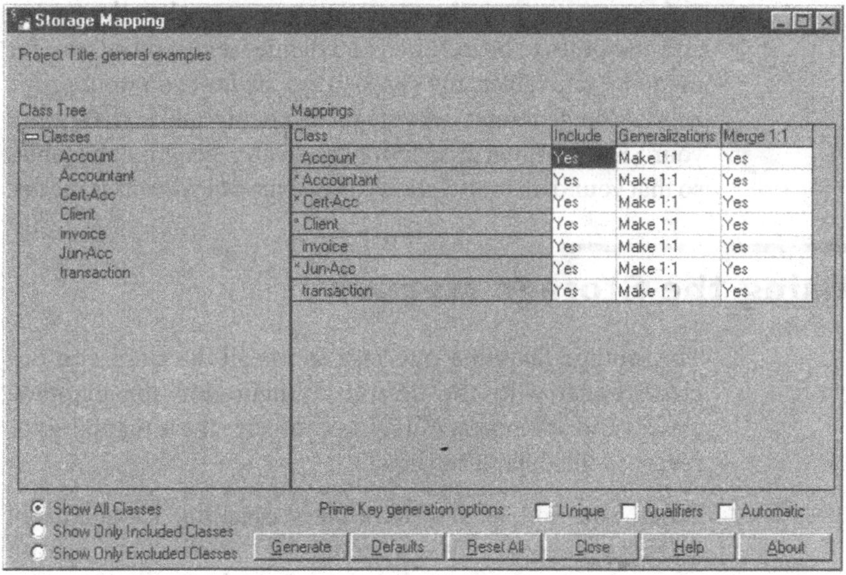

Figure 9.1 The Storage Mapper.

The Storage Mapper populates our model with tables that contain columns and relationships derived from class diagrams. By using the Storage Mapper, we ensure that there is consistency between classes and tables within a model. The generated tables can then be used to develop table diagrams.

Once the storage items have been generated and added to the dictionary, we can add them to a table relationships diagram. The Storage Mapper maps the items in a class model to data model items, as shown in Table 9.1.

Table 9.1 Mapping of class diagram elements to storage items.

Class model item	Storage item
Class	Table
Link class (i.e. collection class)	Table
Association	Relationship
Aggregation	Relationship
Attribute	Column

Before you generate the mappings, you can select the classes and attributes to be included and define storage properties for mapping into tables. You can also specify how you want prime keys to be generated. If you subsequently make changes to your SELECT Enterprise model, you can regenerate the tables so that your data model stays consistent with your class model.

Using the Storage Mapper

The Storage Mapping interface shows all the classes in our class model with the default configuration for mapping classes and attributes. You can reconfigure these mappings or revert to the default settings.

When you add a class to a class diagram, its persistent property is set to true as a default. This means that you want to store its data, and the class appears in the Storage Mapper. If you do not want a class to persist, you can set the persistent property to false. When we map a class, an asterisk appears by the class name in the Storage Mapping interface.

We can control which attributes are included in the mapping in a similar manner.

Managing Mapping Options

Figure 9.1 shows the Properties for Class dialog of the Storage Mapper. We can use it to specify the following mapping options for a class:

● Include the class in the mapping.
● Specify the generalizations, or inheritance, as one-to-one relationships. We can either include the sub-classes in their super-classes or include the super-classes in their sub-classes. The choice will affect the number of tables that are to be generated.
● Choose to merge one-to-one relationships into the same table.

Similarly you use the Properties for Attribute dialog to specify the following mapping options for an attribute:

Include the attribute in the mapping.

- Include the attribute in the main table.
- Change the name of the column.
- Change the name of the table.

If your knowledge of relational databases is a little rusty, you will find it useful to read Chapter 14, especially the section on converting an OO design into a relational database design. The Storage Mapper can be used to do this conversion automatically.

Managing Prime Keys

A prime key is an important concept of relational databases. If you convert classes to tables and attributes to columns you are effectively generating a relational database and you need to specify a prime key for each table. A unique attribute is a suitable candidate for a prime key column. You could also use multiple attributes to form a prime key. When we add a new attribute to a class in a class diagram it has, by default, its unique storage value set to false. We can change this to true by selecting Unique in the attribute Options tab to indicate that the attribute uniquely defines the instance of the class. Once we do that we will see the attribute in the Storage Mapper interface with the prefix [u].

You have to choose from three options when generating the prime key: Unique, Qualifiers, and Automatic. You can generate prime keys from unique attributes or qualified attributes. If we want to generate a prime key from multiple attributes, we use non-unique attributes. In this case we have the responsibility of defining the columns as prime key manually. The Automatic option will automatically generate the prime key from the table name.

Data dictionary

Every model within SELECT Enterprise has a data dictionary. You can add new items directly to the dictionary and, generally, every new item you add to a diagram is automatically added to the dictionary.

According to the way you want to work, you can use either the Dictionary or the Relationships tab of the Explorer window to review and access the dictionary items.

SELECT Enterprise provides you with tools to perform tasks on the dictionary as a whole, for example you can generate reports and configure the model template to suit your requirements.

Checking consistency

SELECT Enterprise provides us with the tools to check the consistency between the components of our diagrams such as classes and their relationships, which may appear in both class and collaboration diagrams.

To check the consistency of individual components, select the diagram that contains that component, and then select the component that you want to check. Right-click and select Report | Consistency from the drop down menu as shown in Figure 9.2.

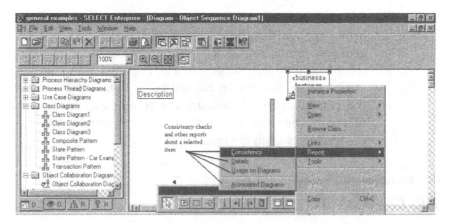

Figure 9.2 Generating reports on a component.

If the item passes the consistency checks that means we have used the item in a consistent way. Other reports, such as Usage On Diagrams and Details, are useful to view how you used the item and therefore to check the correctness of the modelling. We may use the item consistently but on the wrong diagrams or with the wrong details.

We can also check consistency by selecting the Tools | Report Writer menu option. The Report Writer dialog box is shown in Figure 9.3.

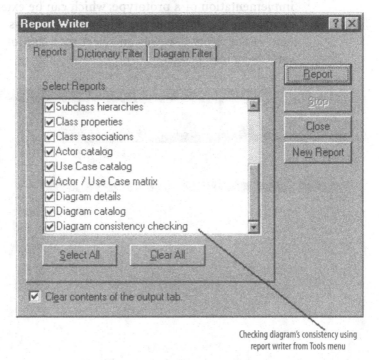

Checking diagram's consistency using report writer from Tools menu

Figure 9.3 The Report Writer dialog.

Select the Diagram consistency checking option and generate the report. Usually it generates the report for all the diagrams, but we can filter the output by using Dictionary Filter to specify which dictionary items we want. This will give us an item-based report, which is similar to the individual checking approach but with the flexibility of including multiple items. We can also filter the output by using `Diagram Filter`, to choose which diagrams are checked.

Code generators

SELECT Enterprise provides us with code generation tools that allow us to automatically generate C/C++ and SQL code from a design. These are very useful for a fast implementation of a prototype, which can be extended to a complete implementation. Figure 9.4 shows the `C++ Generator`. Note that we can select the class for which we want to generate code.

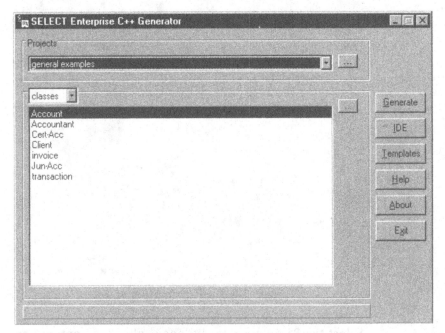

Figure 9.4 *The C++ Code Generator.*

Figure 9.5 shows us the `SQL Schema Generator`, which allows us to generate SQL statements for our tables. The use of SQL generator with `Storage Mapper` enables us to develop databases from our models fast and efficiently and for a choice of database environments. The one shown in Figure 9.5 is for Oracle.

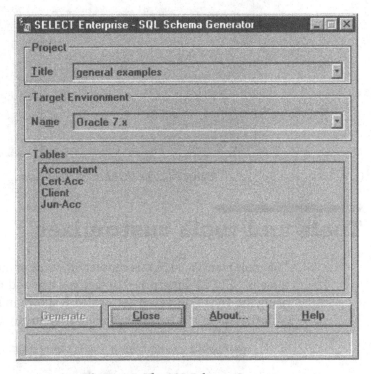

Figure 9.5 The SQL Schema Generator.

Additionally, SELECT Enterprise provides a CORBA IDL Generator, shown in Figure 9.6, for more advanced database development using the CORBA common architecture. CORBA is covered in Chapter 14 and common architectures in Chapter 16.

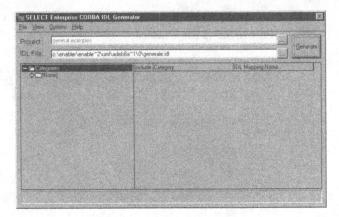

Figure 9.6 The CORBA IDL Generator.

Tools and tools customizer

The tools mentioned in this chapter are some of the available tools in SELECT Enterprise. In fact you can add more tools using the `Tools Customizer`, which is shown in Figure 9.7. Note that some of these tools you may need to buy as add-ons.

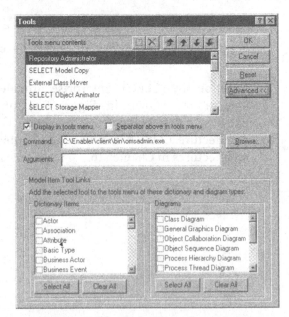

Figure 9.7 The Tools Customizer window.

Chapter 10

Patterns

In addition to UML (and) [illegible] some examples from two of about books, these [illegible] we taken from COAD and OO patterns. As every they [illegible] well known. In OAD details references. See First, about [illegible] the following comments [illegible]

- Adapter is a class [illegible]
- Observer is a[illegible]
- Bridge combines [illegible]

Introduction

Patterns are an important subject for both researchers and practitioners in OO analysis and design (OOAD). The identification and use of patterns in systems analysis and design practices has attracted a lot of interest recently. The results of this work are being rapidly adopted by OOAD practitioners. Many of the current advances such as component software and common architectures are attributed to patterns research and development. In this chapter we will look at the two types of patterns:

● Analysis patterns
● Design patterns

In addition, we will study briefly some examples of analysis and design patterns that are taken from OOAD and OO patterns literature. There are many patterns in OOAD literature therefore we have chosen only the following common examples:

● Analysis: transaction patterns
● Design: state patterns
● Design: composite patterns

Analysis Patterns

The analysis stage of software development is concerned with identifying what is happening in the system that we are trying to model. The result usually comes in the form of requirements, both functional and non-functional, that are linked together. The design needs to find ways to build these requirements into a computer system.

If you analyze enough systems, you will find that there are many similarities between different systems. For example, if you analyze bank accounts, Web-based user portals and club membership systems you will find yourself dealing with accounts. Each account needs opening and operating functions of some sort. Also each account will need to record information about the owner or member associated with the account and to keep a record of activities of some sort. They may look different at first but they are all based on similar accounting operations. The details of each accounting system, in terms of design and implementation, however, are different.

If we identify a pattern of similarity during the analysis stage, we refer to it as an analysis pattern. As an example of analysis patterns, we will study transaction patterns.

A transaction pattern is found in a variety of systems. If, for example, you collect several receipts or invoices from different sources, e.g. pharmacy receipt and a supermarket or departmental store receipt, there are common elements in all of them. Once we start writing down the common elements, we find that each of them has:

- A date
- The store name
- A total and maybe subtotals
- A set of one or more transactions.

They may have other details depending on where the receipt came from, but all of them share these basic pieces of information. Now let us look at these pieces of information from another point of view. You will find the date, store name and totals are usually printed once either at the top or the bottom of the receipt. Transactions on the other hand may be repeated depending on how many things you bought or services you received. Figure 10.1 shows us the abstract class diagram of the invoice.

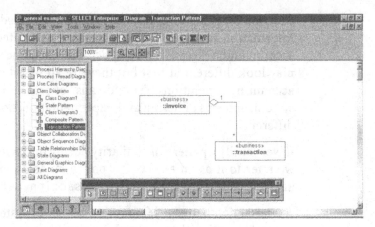

Figure 10.1 A transaction pattern.

The *Invoice* class contains the information that appears once on the invoice such as date and total, while the *Transaction* class contains the information about each transaction. Note the aggregation relationship between *Invoice* class and *Transaction* class to indicate that each invoice may be aggregated from several transactions.

Design patterns

Just as analysis patterns are discovered during the analysis stage, design patterns are discovered during the design stage. As we know, design is concerned with finding solutions for building the system and how the system requirements are going to be achieved.

State patterns

A state pattern is a design pattern that emphasizes the behaviour of a given class. We may find a class that behaves in different ways depending on the state of the class. Let us, for example, take a car rental system where we have a class named *Car*. The states of this class or the objects of this class may indicate whether a *Car* object is:

- Currently rented
- Available
- In for repair
- Booked awaiting collection.

This is shown using the state pattern in Figure 10.2.

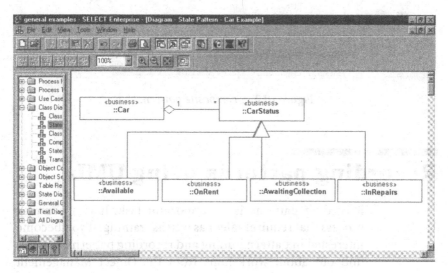

Figure 10.2 A state pattern.

Composite patterns

A `composite pattern` is one that combines a number of objects and then allows us to treat them as a group. This is similar to a drawing program that allows you to insert shapes and then select them to form a group; once you have grouped them you have created one entity that can be moved as a whole. A composite pattern using the graphics example is shown in Figure 10.3.

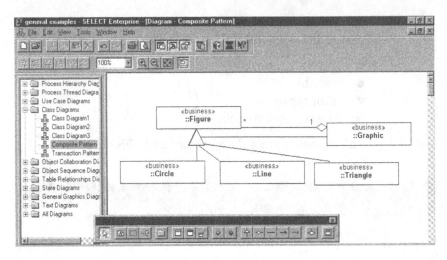

Figure 10.3 A composite pattern.

Recording patterns using UML

Recording patterns is an important task. It is a complex process that requires talent as well as training. If you become interested in pattern mining and recording patterns, you can find out about workshops from the Object Management Group (OMG).

You may like to record some interesting analysis and design patterns in your company for future use. I developed the following method to record patterns using UML rather than the more academic methods of recording patterns.

For analysis patterns, follow these steps:

1. Create a new model. Assign a meaningful name to the model that reflects the pattern name or nature.
2. Create use cases that are the basis of the pattern.
3. Create the class diagram of the pattern.
4. Create collaboration diagrams, sequence diagrams, and state transition diagrams as necessary.
5. Maintain all the diagrams as simple and abstract.
6. Create examples of use.

For design patterns, follow these steps:

1. Create a new model. Assign a meaningful name to the model that reflects the pattern name or nature.
2. Use text diagrams to record which design problem or decision this pattern resolves or presents.
3. Create use cases that are the basis of the pattern
4. Create the class diagram of the pattern showing the structure, the associations, and some attributes.
5. Create collaboration diagrams or sequence diagrams as necessary.
6. Create state transition diagrams detailing the solution the pattern presents to the given problem.
7. Create examples of use.

In some cases you may not need to follow all these steps. Over time you may generate your own protocol of recording patterns.

Chapter
11

Analysis to Design

Introduction

The difference between analysis and design is similar to the difference between an architect's drawings and an interior designer's drawings. The architect tells us the number of rooms, the distribution and functions of these rooms, and so on. The interior designer however tells us more about material, colour and how the design will be done. The analyst is the architect who tells us *what* we need, while the designer is equivalent to the interior designer who tells us *how* to achieve what we need in more detail. UML uses this analogy in providing us with analysis and design tools.

In UML, the design is an extension of the analysis. In other words, the diagrams we used for analysis will be used in design in extended formats. Therefore, this chapter does not introduce new diagrams. Instead, it shows how the diagrams we have studied so far can be used in design, emphasizing that analysis and design are not separate within OO methodologies. In this chapter we will look at:

- Essential and real use cases
- Class diagrams and design class diagrams
- Extended interaction diagrams
- Extended behavioural diagrams
- How SELECT enables and supports these features

Essential and real use cases

The use cases we have created in the analysis stage would not usually contain extensive information on the working of the system. As you develop your models further you get to know more about the system you are trying to design. This familiarity with the system is reflected in the expansion of use cases to contain more details.

The use cases that are created during analysis are called essential use cases, because they contain only the essential information. The use cases that are developed during design are called real use cases because they represent the physical working of the system in the real world. To explain this difference let us look at the following example. Let us assume that we are withdrawing money from a cash dispenser. The essential use case in textual view would be:

```
Use case name: withdraw money
Actor: customer
Description:
  System: requests identification
  Customer: identifies itself
  System: provides options
  Customer: requests money
Use Case Ends
```

However, when we look at the actual working of the system, the customer needs to insert a card and tap in the PIN. The real use case that describes this may be in the following form:

```
Use case name: withdraw money
Actor: customer
Description:
  System: requests identification
  Customer: presents a bankcard
  System: prompts for PIN
  Customer: taps in the PIN
  System: provides options
  Customer: chooses Withdrawal option
  System: presents Withdrawal screen
  Customer: taps in the amount
  System: dispenses the money
  System: provides option of exiting
  Customer: requests exit option or another service
Use Case Ends
```

Design class diagram

The class diagram is the most important diagram we develop during analysis and design. In fact, the class diagram will be used at every step of our software development. As a result, we will re-use the abstract class diagram we develop during analysis and extend it into a design class diagram. We do this by extending the classes to include:

● All their attributes and their types
● All methods, their types and their parameters or arguments
● Interface classes
● Data management classes.

Once we reach a full design class diagram, the implementation, especially in object-oriented languages such as Java, becomes a straightforward job. As an example, let us take the *Account* class from Chapter 6 (see Figure 11.1) and see how we extend it to a design class diagram.

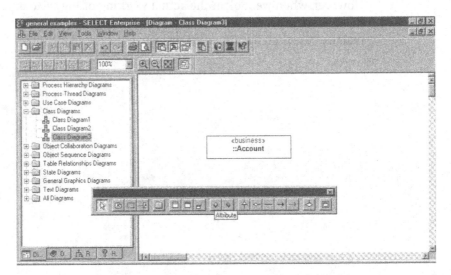

Figure 11.1 The abstract Account class.

If you review Chapter 6, you will find that we added some attributes and methods to this class. The class diagram we created then is shown in Figure 11.2.

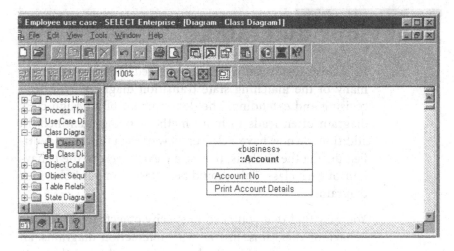

Figure 11.2 *The* Account class in more detail.

Sometimes during analysis you may find that you need to add some attributes and methods to existing classes. This is not wrong. In fact, this is one of the advantages of using an OO approach and a CASE tool. However when we get to the design phase we have to make sure that all the requirements of design are represented. In other words, the classes must be ready to be implemented.

Let us consider the design requirements that are missing from the *Account* class in its present form. You may notice first that there are some attributes missing. What do you think are the attributes that are needed?

Interaction diagrams

Interaction diagrams are extended in similar way to the class diagrams. At the design stage, we have more information and knowledge about the system and its functionality. This should be reflected in the interaction diagrams. This means we may have to specify objects, as objects of the same class may interact with each other.

Behaviour diagrams

It is clear that, once we have extended the class diagram, many of the matching state transition diagrams will need revising and extending. The development of a design class diagram often leads to more methods being identified. In addition, we now have a clearer view of each function identified during the analysis; that is, a clearer view of the behaviour of each class. This should be reflected in our behaviour diagrams.

You may find that you need to specify objects to extend the behaviour diagrams. Just as with interaction diagrams, an object of the class for which you are developing the state transition diagram may interact with other objects from the same class or with objects from other classes. The steps of modelling behaviour for design are the same as presented in Chapter 8.

SELECT Enterprise support for design expansion

As we have seen object-oriented analysis and design is a recursive process. You use more or less the same diagrams during analysis and design, some of which, such as class diagrams, last the full life cycle of the software that is being developed. This provides a strong argument for CASE tools such as SELECT Enterprise. As you have already seen, you can edit and expand the abstract diagrams that you build during analysis into full design diagrams without the need to rebuild them. In fact, the design process becomes an extension of the analysis process as more information is added to our diagrams and models. In addition, as we have seen in Chapter 9, SELECT Enterprise provides us with further tools to produce reports, check consistency between diagrams and prototype a system easily and fast.

Chapter 12

Domain Modelling

Introduction

Domain modelling is an important part of systems analysis and design. I like to compare it to architectural blue prints, which the architect prepares before any construction takes place. There are several aspects of domain modelling, some of which are employed during requirements capture and analysis while other parts come at a later stage of the design. In this chapter we will look at:

- Domain modelling
- Package diagrams
- Process hierarchy diagrams
- Process thread diagrams.

Domain modelling

Domain modelling is a term that has a variety of meaning, but it is most commonly used to mean a high-level model of the whole system. The domain model may represent the organization, with the business processes modelled using process hierarchy and thread diagrams. Alternatively, the domain model may represent the architectural organization of the software, modelled using package diagrams.

Modern systems are usually developed in tiers. Some common tiered architectures are shown in Figure 12.1. The most widely used is the three-tier architecture, however, in some cases, more than three tiers are used. Many older systems still in use were modelled as two-tier systems. We can use the general graphics facility available in SELECT Enterprise to draw the system architecture.

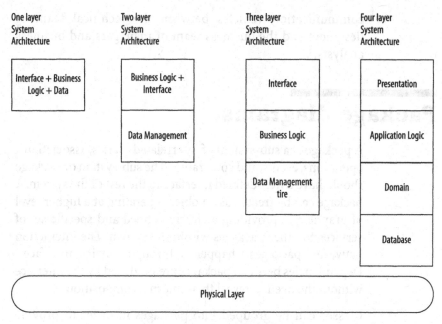

Figure 12.1 Tiered architectures

Once we have identified the tiers we need to break each tier into modules. Identifying modules may best be done in collaboration with the end users and derived from the system requirements.

SELECT Enterprise provides us with package diagrams to show the sub-systems partitioning of the system we are developing. Package diagrams can also be used to show the vertical partitioning of a layer in the system architecture. Package diagrams are used in the development of software technical specifications during analysis and design.

SELECT Enterprise also provides us with process hierarchy diagrams and process thread diagrams to model business organization processes. These two diagrams are the basics of the Business Process Modelling (BPM) provided by SELECT Enterprise, which allows us to model information about a business in terms of its organizational infrastructure, its business processes and the users of those business processes. These diagrams, unlike package diagrams, are created in requirements gathering and analysis and can be used as communication vehicles between the technical team of designers and the business team of managers and business analysts.

Package diagrams

A package is a sub-system of interrelated classes, associations, operations, events, and constraints. The sub-system or package should have a well-defined interface to the rest of the system. A package can be treated as an object operating at a higher level of granularity, providing a clearly defined and specific set of services to other packages within the system. The interaction between packages happens through their interfaces. Dependencies between packages are modelled by the interface without the need to reveal their internal composition.

Classes can be grouped into packages in order to provide consistent business services to meet the specific requirements of business processes. This enables the abstraction of complex interactions that may take place at the class level. Packages can also provide services across system tiers in support of a service-based architecture.

Figure 12.2 shows a package that contains several user classes. This package forms a user interface component of our system (see Chapter 13).

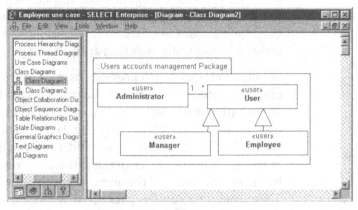

Figure 12.2 A package diagram.

We can perform the following tasks to build the package diagram:

- Add a package.
- Link a package to other dictionary items.
- Relate one package to another with a dependency.
- Add other items such as classes, user classes, and associations. In other words, a package can contain a full class diagram, as shown in Figure 12.2.
- Edit the package through the properties window.

Process hierarchy diagrams

Process hierarchy diagrams (PHDs) are specific to SELECT Enterprise and do not appear in commonly used UML documentation. A process hierarchy diagram is used to capture and graphically display the relationship between the levels of process granularity. At the very top we find the business organization, an enterprise or part of an enterprise, which is under study. This is divided into key business processes consisting of process groups. Process groups can be nested as required depending on the size and complexity of the enterprise we are modelling. A process group consists of Elementary Business Processes (EBPs) and other process groups. They can be re-used both within and across process threads. Figure 12.3 shows an example of a process hierarchy diagram.

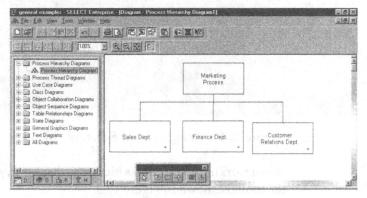

Figure 12.3 A process hierarchy diagram.

Business processes in PHDs are mapped to use cases and associated with actors. Actors, which are referred to as "business actors" in the context of a PHD, perform business processes. Actors and use cases do not appear on a PHD but we can edit them from the Dictionary window or use case diagrams.

A business process marked with an asterisk is an elementary business process, which is a leaf node that has no child processes. We can divide an elementary process into business steps. This is done in SELECT Enterprise by modelling it as a process thread diagram.

Creating a process hierarchy diagram

We create a process hierarchy diagram in the same way we created all other diagrams. When you right-click, you see the menu in Figure 12.4.

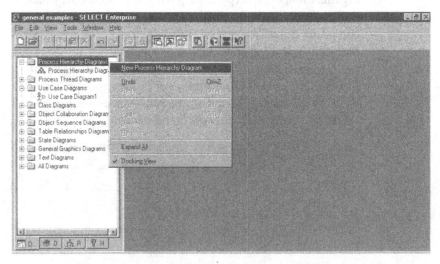

Figure 12.4 Creating a process hierarchy diagram.

When working with process hierarchy diagrams, you can use the toolbox shown in Figure 12.5.

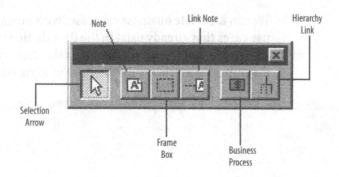

Figure 12.5 *The process hierarchy diagram toolbox.*

Editing a process hierarchy diagram

When we edit a process hierarchy diagram, we use the Properties window, shown in Figure 12.6, to change the settings as needed.

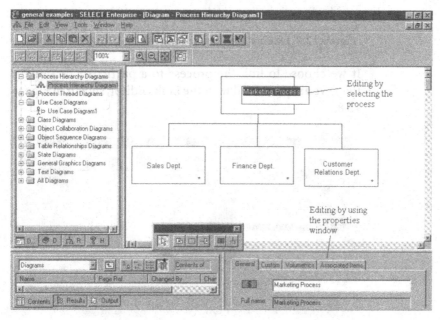

Figure 12.6 *Editing a process hierarchy diagram.*

We can associate business processes with business actors and use cases that already exist in the data dictionary. Figure 12.7 shows the choice of linking to data dictionary items or diagrams for a process on the PHD in Figure 12.6.

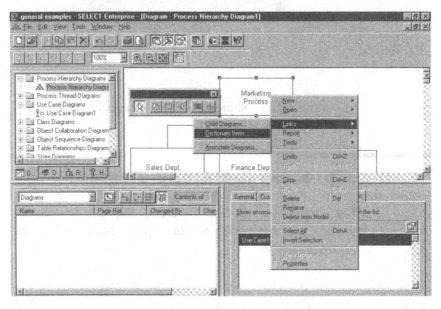

Figure 12.7 Linking a process to a dictionary item.

If we choose to link the process to a particular dictionary item, we are presented with the Links Editor, shown in Figure 12.8.

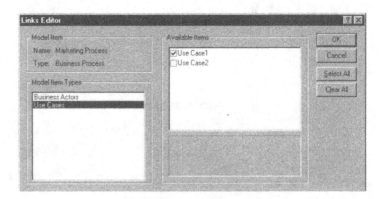

Figure 12.8 The links editor.

After choosing the dictionary item in Figure 12.8, it appears in the properties window (see Figure 12.9).

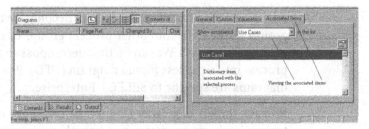

Figure 12.9 The properties window of a linked use case.

Linking business processes

To link two processes, click the `Hierarchy Link` button in the toolbox and then bring together the required items on the diagram with the constructed link as in Figure 12.10.

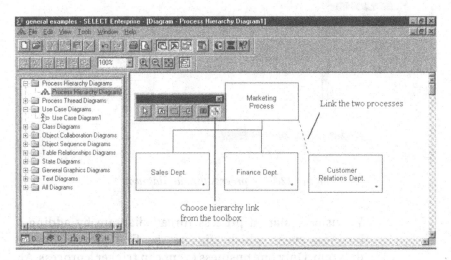

Figure 12.10 Linking two processes.

Process thread diagrams

As we have mentioned earlier, we can decompose the process groups of the PHD into other process groups or elementary business processes. We can further decompose each business process into a process thread diagram (PTD). Process thread diagrams are specific to SELECT Enterprise.

Process thread diagrams (Figure 12.11) show how events trigger business processes and how these processes in turn trigger other processes. Events can be internal or external. The thread terminates in one or more results. A result is a view of an internal event.

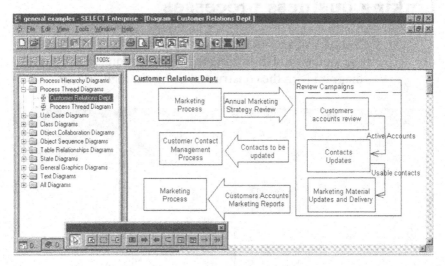

Figure 12.11 A process thread diagram.

We usually start a process thread diagram by adding a business event, which triggers the first process on the diagram. Only one business event can trigger a process. An event also resumes the process after it has been suspended by a process break. After we have added events, we may add the business process that is triggered by the event. We can use transitions to link items on a process thread diagram.

Creating a process thread diagram

We can create a PTD in the same way we create other diagrams, by right-clicking (see Figure 12.12).

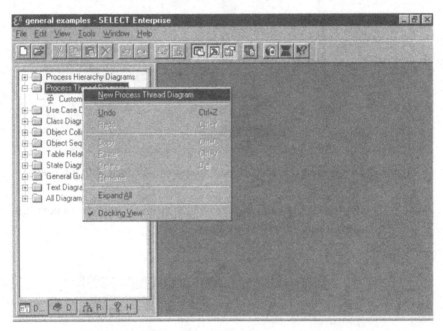

Figure 12.12 Creating a process thread diagram.

Alternatively, we can associate the PTD with a process in a PHD, as a child diagram (see Figure 12.13). This is very similar to what we have done with state diagrams in Chapter 8.

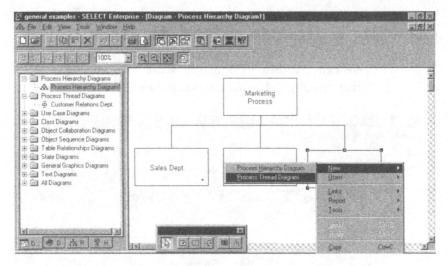

Figure 12.13 Creating a process thread diagram associated with a process.

Figure 12.14 shows the PTD toolbox, which makes the development of PTDs easier.

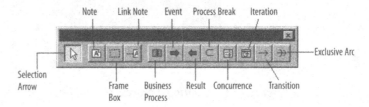

Figure 12.14 The process thread diagram toolbox.

Editing a process thread diagram

When we edit a process thread diagram, we use the properties window to change the settings as needed. In addition, we can associate actors and use cases that already exist in the dictionary with the business process, following these steps:

1. In the Dictionary window, expand the business process model, then right-click on the process with which you want to associate the actors and use cases.

2. Choose the Associate Diagram option to display the Create Associations **dialog.**
3. Select the Actors or Use Cases options.

Adding a process

A process represents a business activity to accomplish a business requirement. We add a process to a process thread diagram in a similar manner to adding elements to other diagrams. Figure 12.15 shows the use of the right mouse button; the other method is to use the toolbox.

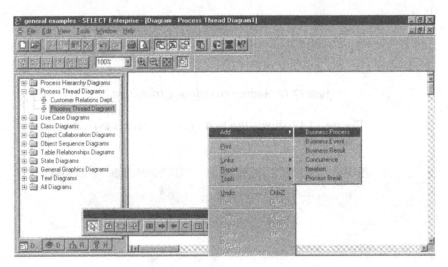

Figure 12.15 Adding a process to PTD.

Using transitions

Transitions are a means of linking processes and moving between them. However, SELECT Enterprise distinguishes between transitions, which are methods executed, and events, or external stimuli.

We add a transition by clicking on the process thread diagram toolbox and joining the required items on the diagram with the transition. Figure 12.16 shows the ordinary transitions we use to link elements within a PTD.

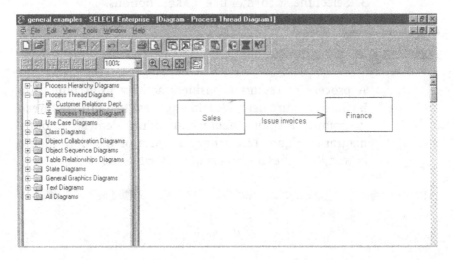

Figure 12.16 Adding an ordinary transition.

Figure 12.17 shows the two types of events available: Event and Result Event.

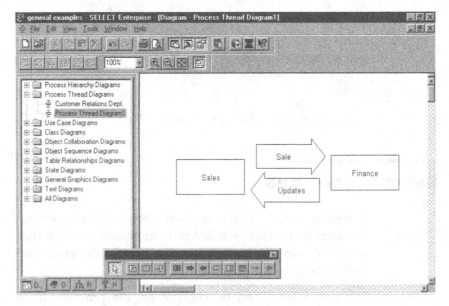

Figure 12.17 Adding events and results as transitions.

Adding an exclusive arc transition

We can add an exclusive arc to specify a delay or a percentage split for the transition, or to make the transition optional. Figure 12.8 shows an exclusive arc as an optional split of the original transition.

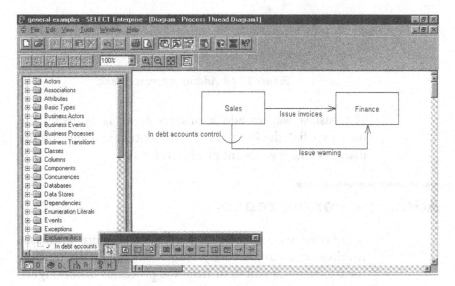

Figure 12.18 Adding the exclusive arc transition.

Adding a process break

We can use a process break to temporarily suspend a thread. A process break can occur, for example, when the process has to wait for another event before it can complete. Figure 12.19 shows the use of a process break initiated from the *Finance* process that indicates there is a *Debt* that may stop the proposed sale, which was initiated by the *Sale* process.

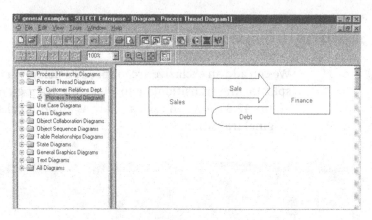

Figure 12.19 Adding a process break.

The easiest way to add a process break is by using the toolbox. Click the `Process break` button and click on the diagram where you want to add the break.

Adding a concurrence

A concurrence indicates that the two or more processes within it occur concurrently. Transitions can flow to or from the concurrence and to or from the processes inside. Figure 12.20 shows the insertion of a concurrence in a PTD.

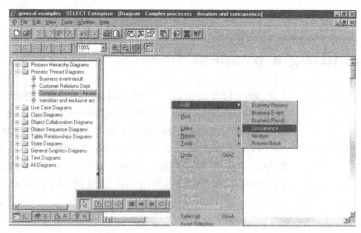

Figure 12.20 Adding a concurrence process.

As Figure 12.21 shows, the *Customer accounts review* and the *Contacts updates* processes happen concurrently.

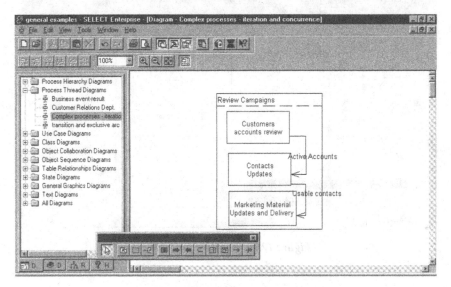

Figure 12.21 Concurrent processes.

We can add events, results, and iterations to a concurrence. We can also have one concurrence inside another, producing a nested concurrence.

Adding an iteration

An iteration process indicates that the processes within it are repeated. Iteration is very similar to concurrence, in that we can add events, other iterations, concurrences and so on. Figure 12.22 shows an example of iteration where the reviews happen over and over again based on preset time milestones.

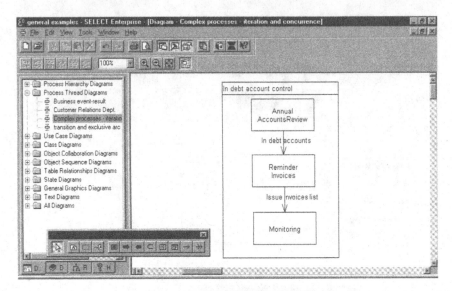

Figure 12.22 *Iterative processes.*

Chapter 13

User Interface Design

Introduction

It is a good idea to leave user interface design until most of the other design aspects are completed. User interface classes are additional classes that will not affect the internal processing but will provide communication points for the users to interact with the system. Interface classes are usually grouped together in packages to provide a separate layer from the business classes in the system architecture. In this chapter we will look at:

● Deriving user interface classes
● User interface design.

Deriving user interface classes

The first step in developing user interfaces within object-oriented modelling is to derive the required classes. To do this we need to go back to our use cases and identify the users. It helps to use the actors that appear in the use cases as an indication of which users are going to use the system.

The second step is to identify who needs to know what. In single-user systems or where different users may use the same interface this is not a problem and we use one user interface design for all of them. However, in many business systems, users will need different screens with different functions that are related to their jobs. This means we have to have different user interfaces.

The third step is to identify which business class is holding the required information. In other words, which internal classes require interface classes. This step will also enable us to identify the associations between user interface classes and business classes.

Finally, we have to decide the content of each user interface class. To do this, we may elect to use prototyping, as we discuss later on within this chapter.

User interface design

Adding user interface classes is part of generating the design class diagram from the abstract model. We have already seen how to convert a class diagram into a design class diagram. In some cases, adding user interface classes to the design class diagram is enough, as is the case with small projects and systems that would have limited user interaction such as machinery control systems. However in business-based applications, the user interface is an important aspect of the system and therefore we need to look at it in further detail.

There are three ways to model and deal with the user interface:

- Adding user interface classes
- Using user interface packages
- Prototyping

Adding user interface classes

User interfaces can be represented within a class diagram in two ways. The first approach is to include the interface within the class for which the interface is developed. This means that elements of the user interface are attributes of the class. Figure 13.1 shows the interface elements with which a user can interact with the *Account* class.

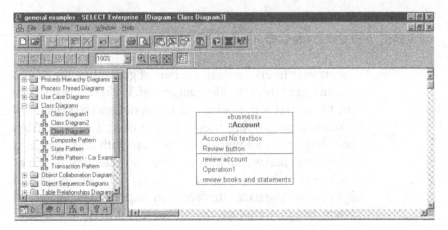

Figure 13.1 Account *class with embedded interface elements.*

The second approach is to separate the user interface from the class. In other words, we include a separate class that is usually referred to as a user interface class. Figure 13.2 shows an example of the *Account* class with its own user interface class attached.

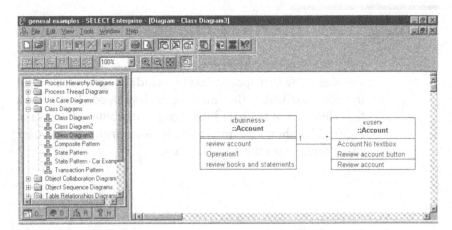

Figure 13.2 Account *class and* Account Interface *class.*

The disadvantage of combining the interface with the class is that any change to the interface will affect the business classes, which is not the case if they are separate. In addition, the combined class does not support the three-tier architecture model.

The disadvantage of a separate interface class for each class with which the user needs to interact is that it may not be suitable for many databases and Internet based systems.

In SELECT Enterprise, we can model interface classes as user classes. This enables us to model the roles of users and hence provide each user with a different interface. In addition to that, the interface classes can be associated with more than one business class, which means that we do not need to create as many interface classes as business classes. This may lead to a reduction in the number of classes in our design model and hence better performance.

Using User Interface Packages

The use of user classes brings us to the second approach to user design, which is using ready-made packages. These packages can be user classes we have grouped into a package separate from our business model design or they may be provided by a third party as is the case with the Java Swing library. The design of a user interface may affect and be affected by the control model we use. It might be useful to have a look at the control models in Chapter 16.

We can model the user interface as a package or re-usable component. To do so we use package diagrams. Figure 13.3 shows an example of using the Java Swing package.

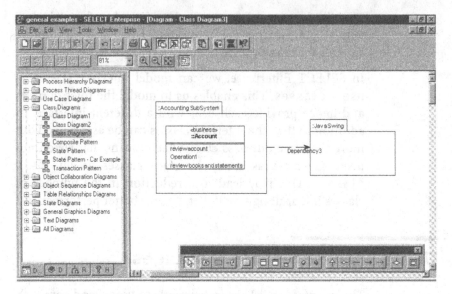

Figure 13.3 Using the Java Swing package.

This technique is very popular especially with programmers who use visual programming languages such as Java, Visual C++ and Visual Basic where interface and graphics libraries are provided. However this technique can be taken further and we can develop our own graphic user interface (GUI) packages.

Note that the use of ready-made packages does not replace the use of interface classes. The only difference in this case is that the user interface class will be a collection or an aggregation of classes within the package.

Prototyping

Prototyping is a valuable tool for user interface design. It enables us to see in advance what the interface may look like and enables easier communication with users. It may be difficult to explain to an accountant that he or she will be using buttons to initiate new accounts and fill in text boxes, but if we use Visual Basic to prototype the user interface screen (see Figure 13.4), it may be much simpler to explain.

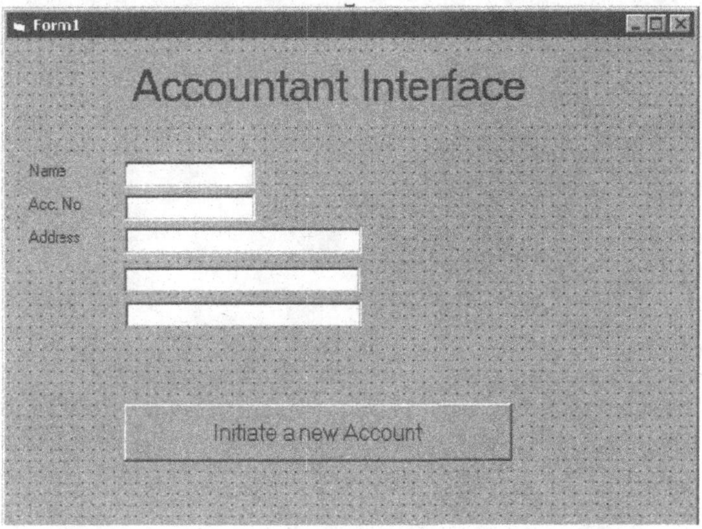

Figure 13.4 *A prototype of a Visual Basic interface screen.*

This technique helps us to identify the user interface classes as well as their components. This is then reflected in the aggregation used to build the user interface class, when using ready-made packages.

Chapter 14

Database Modelling

Introduction

Handling data efficiently is a central part of most applications. We need to maintain, organize, and search through data. To enable these operations to be done effectively, we use databases. Data is very important and, as a result, the development of database administration systems is far advanced. Most of these systems, however, are based on relational databases. In Chapter 9, we saw the `Storage Mapper` facility in SELECT Enterprise that enables us to convert our class diagrams to databases. In this chapter we will look at:

- Types of databases
- Table diagrams
- Editing a table
- Relationships
- Converting an OO design into a relational database design
- CORBA and ORB patterns

Types of databases

Different modelling techniques lead to different types of databases. The most successful and widely used are relational databases, which are based on the concept of building relationships between different sets of data that are saved in the database. Figure 14.1 shows an entity relationship diagram. It shows the database of a vehicle scheduling system. There are entities such as *Vehicle, Journey* and *Route*. These entities relate to each other with different types of relationships. For example, each vehicle may take different routes in its journeys. At the same time, each route may be taken by several vehicles.

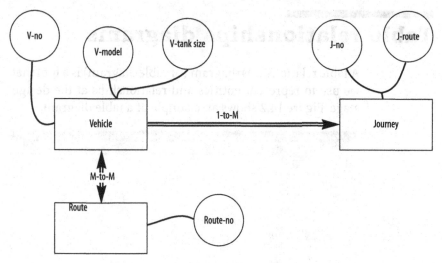

Figure 14.1 An entity relationship diagram

The circles attached to each entity are some possible attributes of that entity. In modern relational database design, entity relationship diagrams do not contain the attributes in this form. Instead, they are accompanied by table description documentation in the form of:

```
Vehicle (V-no, V-model, V-tank size)
```

The attribute that is underlined is a distinctive attribute that has unique values. We refer to this attribute as the primary key. In SELECT Enterprise, we use table diagrams to present database design.

Another type of database is an object-oriented database. OO databases are still being developed and OO database administration systems are not as well developed as those of relational databases. Some languages, such as Smalltalk and Java provide, basic database administration functions. Many OO systems use relational database administration systems for the data layer or the data sub-system in the physical layer. In many cases, an extra interface layer is used between the business layer or logic layer and the data layer. This interface is usually known as middleware.

Table relationships diagrams

A table relationships diagram (or table diagram) is a tool that we use to represent entities and relationships at the design stage. Figure 14.2 shows an example of a table diagram.

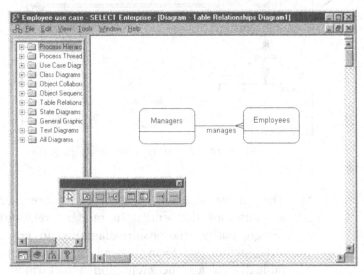

Figure 14.2 A table diagram.

In a table diagram we can use entities, relationships and entity attributes. Since a table diagram is a design diagram, SELECT Enterprise does not provide many-to-many relationships and they must be resolved before the development of table diagrams. Since we will use table diagrams to design databases, the design issues and decisions will be made while we are moving from analysis to design and will usually be reflected in the design class diagram. The table diagram will be based on the design class diagram.

Creating a table diagram

Creating a table diagram is similar to creating any other diagram. Figure 14.3 shows how to right-click to create a table diagram from the drop down menu.

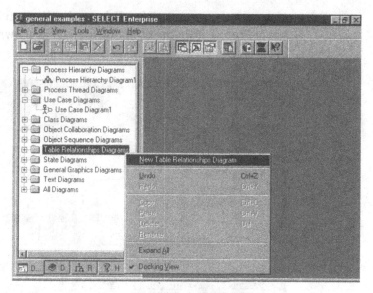

Figure 14.3 Creating a table diagram.

Adding a Table

Once we have started a new table diagram, we can add a new table using the toolbox, which is shown in Figure 14.4.

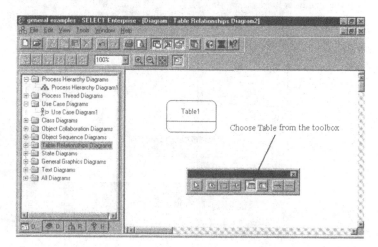

Figure 14.4 Creating a table using the toolbox.

Alternatively, we can right-click on the diagram and select
Add | Table from the drop down menu as shown in Figure
14.5.

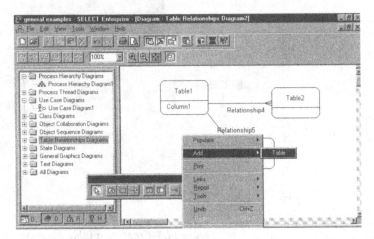

Figure 14.5 Creating a table using the drop down menu.

This method provides us with the choice of either adding a
new table or selecting an existing table. Figure 14.6 shows the
drop down menu with a list of existing tables and the option
to add a new table.

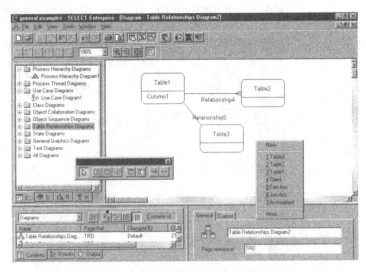

Figure 14.6 Adding a table using the drop down menu.

Deleting a Table

Deleting a table follows the same steps we used to delete elements from other types of diagram in previous chapters. We can either delete the table from the diagram or from the model. Figure 14.7 shows the drop down menu for a selected table.

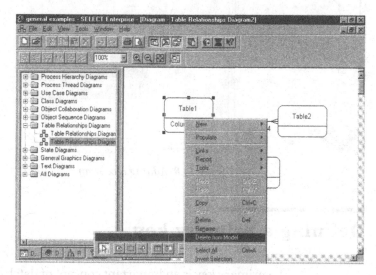

Figure 14.7 Deleting a table.

Editing a table

Editing a table involves several concepts and elements. Adding an attribute to a table is very similar to adding an attribute to a class. However, table attributes are presented as columns. In addition, we have to define a primary key for each table.

Working with Columns

Columns are the attributes of a table. Each record of a table will consist of one or more columns. Figure 14.8 shows a table with one column, and the Column button on the toolbox.

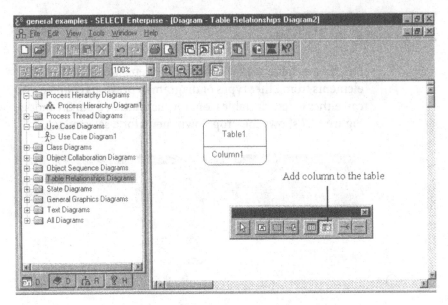

Figure 14.8 Adding a column.

Defining a primary key

The primary key is an important concept of database design. It is an attribute that is guaranteed to have unique values. Each table has to have a primary key.

For example, when you register for a college course, you get a registration number, which identifies your record on the college database. While more than one student may have the same name, every student has a unique student number. Because the student number has unique values, it identifies students individually and can be used as a primary key to find and retrieve records.

Figure 14.9 shows the window we use to edit columns. Right-click on the column you want to edit and select Properties. The properties window usually appears in the lower right corner of the SELECT Enterprise interface.

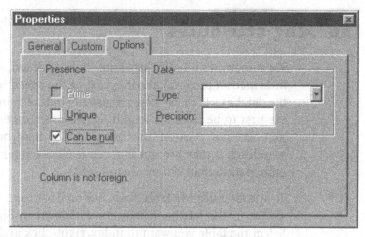

Figure 14.9 The properties window for a column.

In Figure 14.9, notice that the Prime option is not active. This is because we allowed the column to have a null value. If you deselect Can be null, the Prime checkbox becomes active and then we can assign this column as a primary key, as in Figure 14.10.

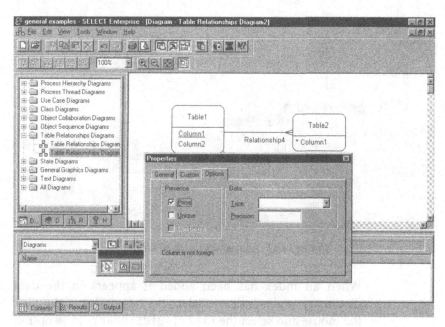

Figure 14.10 Designating a column as the primary key.

Indexing attributes

We sometimes identify attributes to be indexed, to speed up information retrieval at some cost to the speed of updating the database. Primary keys are usually indexed since they are the first to be used for searching. However, other attributes that are not part of the primary key may be used for searching. If they are not indexed it takes longer to retrieve information than if they are indexed.

To add an index to a table, first click on Dictionary and view **Tables** in the left hand window as shown in Figure 14.11. Select the table you want to index, right-click and select New | Index from the drop down menu.

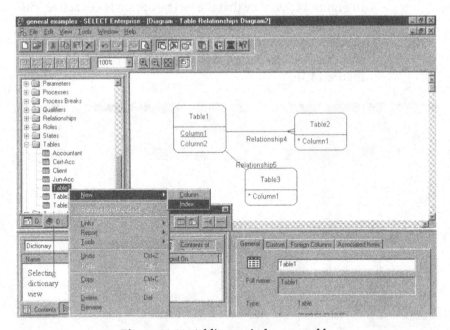

Figure 14.11 Adding an index to a table.

When an index has been added it appears in the data dictionary under indexes. Select the new index, right-click the mouse and select the Link | Dictionary Item option from the drop down menu, as shown in Figure 14.12.

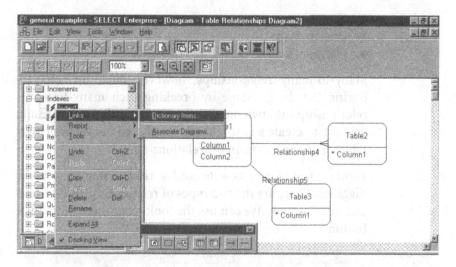

Figure 14.12 Linking a table to a dictionary item.

A Links Editor window will appear. Select the column that you want to index. In Figure 14.13, Column2 has been selected for indexing.

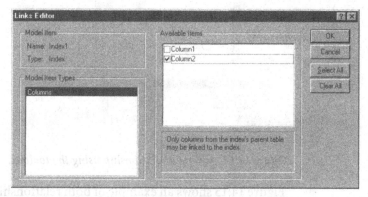

Figure 14.13 Adding a column to an index.

Relationships

Relationships in databases are similar to some of the relationships in class diagrams. There are three types of relationship:

- One-to-one
- One-to-many
- Many-to-many

Many-to-many relationships, however, must be resolved during the design stage by breaking each many-to-many relationship into two one-to-many relationships. As a result we have to create a new table that is shared between the two tables in the many-to-many relationship.

Figure 14.14 shows how to add a relationship in a table diagram. There are the two types of relationship: one-to-one and one-to-many. We can use the toolbox or the right mouse button.

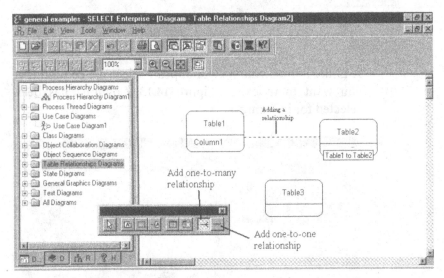

Figure 14.14 Adding a relationship using the toolbox.

Figure 14.15 shows an example of both relationships: one-to-one and one-to-many.

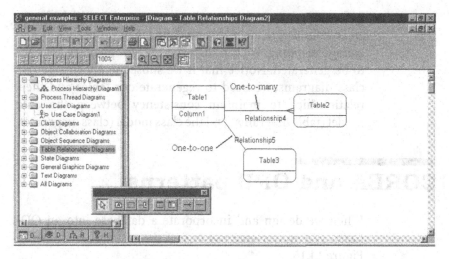

Figure 14.15 One-to-many and one-to-one relationships.

Converting OO design into relational database design

We can use the `Storage Mapper` to automatically generate tables and their relationships based on the information contained in the class diagrams. The tables and relationships are added to the model dictionary. Once the storage items are present in the dictionary, we can add them to a table diagram. By using the SELECT Enterprise `Storage Mapper`, we ensure consistency within a model between class and table diagrams.

When we run the `Storage Mapper`, the items in a class diagram are mapped to the following items in the table diagram:

Table 14.1 Mapping class diagram to relation table diagram

Class diagram elements	Maps to in relational table diagram
Class	Table
Link class	Table
Association	Relationship
Aggregation	Relationship
Attribute	Column

Before we generate the mappings, we can select which classes and attributes are included and define their properties for the storage mapping. We can then specify how primary keys are to be generated. Notice that if we subsequently change our class diagrams, we need to regenerate our tables and their relationships to maintain consistency between the data model (table diagrams) and the class model (class diagrams).

CORBA and ORB patterns

When we design and incorporate a database into an OO-based system, we may use one of the techniques shown in Figure 14.16.

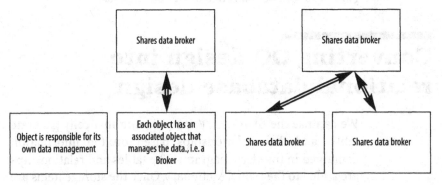

Figure 14.16 Database designs in OO systems

The first technique is the simple technique in which each class is responsible for its data. That means all data management functions such as save, retrieve and sort are part of the class methods. The disadvantage of this technique is that every time we change the database administration system, we have to change the design and implementation of the business classes.

The second technique is to separate the data management functions, by providing a data management class for each business class that requires them. Even though this is a good way of dealing with databases, the increase in the number of classes may slow the system and put pressure on computing resources.

The third technique tries to solve this by providing a general data management class for all business classes. This data management class is often referred to as the Object Broker. It is, in its simplest form, a file management class that enables writing and reading from different files that are associated with the data to be maintained.

The Object Request Broker (ORB) pattern is a design pattern that solves this problem by using both the second and third techniques. The idea behind ORB is to provide a broker that handles all data management requests. In addition, this broker translates between objects and conventional relational database systems. The Common Object Request Broker Architecture (CORBA) is a general architecture for dealing with databases, which is based on ORB. It defines the middleware architecture that resides between business classes, or the logic layer, and database administration systems, which may either be a data layer or a physical layer.

Chapter 15

Completing the Model

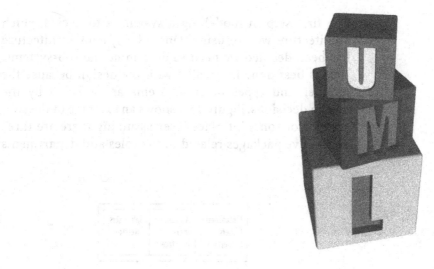

Introduction

In this chapter we will look at what is required to complete our modelling. This chapter provides a summary of supportive elements required during software development. These extra elements are very important and can affect the success of software development projects.

This chapter also provides a summary of the topics which we have covered in this book, before discussing implementation and examples. In this chapter, we will look at:

- Modelling sub-systems
- System modelling views
- Modelling diagrams
- Object-oriented modelling views
- Project management

Modelling sub-systems

The first step in modelling a system is to decide which architecture we are using. Once the system architecture has been decided we need to determine the sub-systems. This is best done in parallel with the design because the number and types of sub-systems are affected by the design decisions. Figure 15.1 shows an example of the sub-systems of some interface layer assuming there are three distinctive packages related to the roles and departments of users.

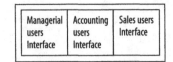

Figure 15.1 Sub-systems of an interface layer.

System modelling views

System modelling views are approaches to system design. They are not solutions in themselves but techniques for looking at the big picture of the system. We can use these techniques in the designing and testing the system under development.

Top-bottom view

In this technique, we start by looking at the whole picture first and then break the system down into smaller parts until we get to the individual classes. This is the best technique if you know little about the domain.

The problem with this technique is the abstraction and generality of the starting point, which may prove to be far from reality. It can lead us in the wrong direction, which means we have to revise our sub-systems design. This technique however is useful when we are deciding which architecture to use.

Bottom-top view

This is the opposite of the top to bottom technique. We start from the bottom, which is usually the individual classes, and we build up sub-systems and then into a full architecture. It is very useful technique if we have lots of knowledge about the domain. The disadvantage of this technique, however, is that the level of detail we are working with may obscure our view of the entire system as one entity. This also may lead us to forget about the architecture decisions, which may force us to accept a de-facto architecture as a result of the design.

Bi-directional view

This technique tries to bring the benefits and reduce the disadvantages of the two previous techniques. In fact, unless you have strong reason to use one of the previous techniques, this would be the technique I would advise you to take. The idea of this technique is to look at both ends of the design process. In other words, we look at the architectural needs of the system as a whole, and at the same time we look at the individual classes.

For example, let us assume we are developing a system for an accounting firm to connect their customers and employees. We meet with the managerial board and gather what they require on a business organizational level from the systems. Then we may meet with individual accountants within the company to define their requirements as individuals dealing with customers and accounts. This will enable us to define the architecture and main functionality of the system and also allow us to define individual components, classes and packages.

Components view

This is a non-traditional view of design and testing, which I have included because of the increasing use of components by system designers. This view would complement any of the other techniques but it works best with bi-directional techniques. The idea is to look at the system as an aggregation of several components. Each component has a clear specification. By selecting the components that satisfy the requirements at hand, we can build our system. These components may be developed in-house or bought from a third party.

Using this view will usually stop us at the architectural and sub-systems level. Once we identify the components that fulfil the requirements, or most of them, we start looking at other parts of the system for which we cannot find ready-made components. We apply other techniques to those parts that need to be specially developed and then build them as sub-systems. In real life, you have to be creative about the development and testing techniques you use.

Modelling diagrams

The modelling diagrams that are used in the completed model may not be restricted to UML diagrams. We may choose to use some conventional diagrams, such as flow charts, during the design of individual classes or methods. In addition, we may use some general graphics diagrams to show the information flow, the operational dependencies or the general architecture of the system.

Object-oriented modelling views

In this section, we will look at two views very often used in OO modelling. These views of design are influenced by the nature of the OO approach.

Responsibility view

This is a behavioural view of the design. It is based on the responsibility of each class and what each class contribute to the working of the full system. Each class should have a precise and clear responsibility. This responsibility can be in the form of operations that the class performs or in the form of maintaining and retrieving data, as is the case with database classes or collection classes. In many cases, the class will have both operational and data-centred responsibilities. However, overloading a class with responsibilities is usually bad design that undermines the benefits and concepts of OO design.

One of the terms often used in association with class responsibility is delegation. This term refers to the situation where a class delegates part or all of a request or operation to another class or group of classes. This happens when the operation the class is trying to execute is out of its functional or data responsibility. Delegation works well and enhances the distributed nature of OO systems; therefore it is becoming a prominent aspect of OO systems.

While the responsibility view is very useful during design in general, it becomes more useful during the design of operations-based systems such as real time and control systems.

Use case view

The use case view is a requirements-based view. It is based on what the user would like the system to do and what a group of classes will contribute to the complete system. This view relies on the use cases developed at the beginning of requirements gathering and analysis. It is useful during the design of user-oriented systems, such as databases.

Project management

Project management is an important part of developing software and systems. It is a key to success, especially in big projects. This is a topic that requires a whole book. However we will look at the basic ideas of project management, which affect the completion of modelling.

Managing time and tasks

Managing time is the most important issue of project and tasks management. There are several approaches to managing.

In time boxing, each task is placed within a time box that usually represents a pre-defined period between two weeks and two months. This pre-defined period may vary from one project to another and can be agreed upon by the project team. Each task has to be done within its respective time box. Once the time given to the task is consumed, the team stops working on that task and moves on to the next one. Figure 15.2 shows an example of time-box task management.

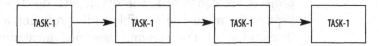

Figure 15.2 The time-boxing technique.

For this technique to work we have to divide the requirements of each task into essential and desirable deliverables. The lost flexibility of time management is compensated by the flexibility in requirements.

There are several other modelling tools that show the scheduling of tasks, such as Pert charts and Gantt charts. Figure 15.4 shows a Gantt chart created using MS Project. Project management tools are especially useful in big projects but are always helpful.

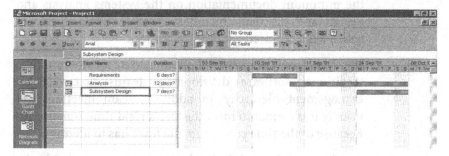

Figure 15.3 A Gantt chart.

Documentation

Documentation is vital for any successful project. Without good documentation any reviewing process becomes almost impossible, since it is not possible to determine whether the project meets the requirements or is on time. If you consider the fact that most OO-based projects rely on prototyping and reviewing the prototyped system, you can appreciate the importance of documentation.

There are two types of documentation as far as OO-based projects are concerned. The developers' documentation is kept to the minimum possible while providing a complete description of the system. User documentation should describe the working of the system and provide as much help as possible in using the system. We do not include anything about the building of the system in the user documentation.

Working in a team

In OO-based projects, the team needs to be working closely together. Many OO-based projects are developed using the Rapid Application Development (RAD) management approach, which relies on time boxing. This means we have the minimum documentation on the systems analysis and design and the team members need to work closely to achieve the required goals of the project.

Working closely empowers the team and its members, unlike traditional software development teams that rely on management hierarchy. In addition, team meetings are usually less formal to meet the task's rigid time constraints. Because of the time constraint, the team has to identify:

- The essential and desirable requirements needed in the system. The essential requirements are those that the system should meet while the desirable requirement are to be achieved as time allows.
- The skills the team has or should have. OO-based projects usually require multi-skilled teams. For an example, the team may include a specialist in databases, another in distributed and remote systems, a Java programmer, and a Web site designer.

Checklist of models

Here is a summary of the diagrams we will normally require:

- Context diagram or general architectural diagrams (this may include components and deployment diagrams)
- Use cases that are developed from essential use cases to real use cases
- A class diagram that is developed from an abstract class diagram to a design class diagram.

In addition, you may need some of the following diagrams:

- Interaction diagrams for some or all use cases
- State diagrams for some or all classes
- Activity diagrams.

In addition to these models we may have extra diagrams associated with some individual methods. Also management charts are required to keep track of the system development. Management charts are usually developed during the requirements analysis.

Chapter 16 · Implementation

Introduction

Once all design models have been completed, it is time to code the system. We have seen that SELECT Enterprise provides us with code generation tools for speedy development. But how are we going to show the relationships between the different pieces of code? How is the control of the system managed? In addition, the system may be required to run on specific hardware or within a specific operating environment, as it is the case with real-time systems. In this chapter we will look at:

- Control techniques
- Component diagrams
- Deployment diagrams.

Control Techniques

Control is a very important issue to be decided on during design and implementation. Usually, control is affected by the system architecture and design decisions. There are two main types of control:

- Centralized
- Distributed

There are also commonly used hybrid control techniques, which are not considered here.

Centralized control

Centralized control is used often in structured programming where there is a single starting point of the system. That starting point is usually presented as a main function that controls the working of the system. Sometimes this technique is used in OO-based systems. We identify a class or an object that will be the main controller of the system. An interface class is often used as a central controller, which controls the initiation and calling of other objects during the running of the system.

Distributed control

Distributed control is more common in OO-based systems than centralized control. It is also commonly used for distributed and network systems such as Internet databases.

The technique is based on the idea that there are no single entry or exit points within the system. In addition, the control of initiating and calling objects is distributed between different objects that may also run on different machines. You can model distributed control by having several interface objects related to different packages or classes. In addition, we can represent distributed control by bi-directional relationships between interface classes or main classes.

Component diagrams

We may look at a `component` as a `package` or a sub-system. However, in UML terms, a component is a distributable piece of software in either source code or executable format. A component is represented in UML by a rectangle with two bars, as shown in figure 16.1.

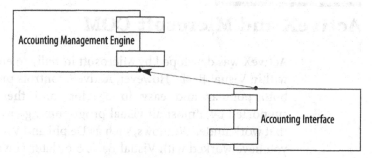

Accounting Management Engine

Accounting Interface

Figure 16.1 A component diagram.

Some of the components may be ready-made components, which we can buy from component providers, such as Component Source. We may also develop components in-house for reuse in different systems.

Reuse and component software

Reuse emerges from the idea of 'why re-invent the wheel?' In other words, if someone else has designed and implemented a component to perform a task why not use that code over and over again whenever that task is to be performed.

Component software is a hot topic within the software development community. In fact, most modern software development uses existing components. The sophistication of software and the similarity between organizations has led to the use of components.

There are several component standards such as ActiveX and Java Beans. In addition, there are common architectures, such as CORBA, which are general designs that are used to develop systems. Many of these common architectures are developed as components and in some cases as stand-alone packages. A look at some Web sites that sell components will give you a better understanding of the component software market. Here we will look briefly at the two common component formats.

ActiveX and Microsoft COM

ActiveX was developed by Microsoft initially to enable reuse within Visual Basic. However, ActiveX controls proved to be both popular and easy to develop, and they are now supported by almost all visual programming environments that work under Windows, such as Delphi and Visual C++. If you have worked with Visual Basic 5 or later you will notice that there are several types of ActiveX projects. There are

ActiveX controls, documents, executables, and dynamic link libraries. While ActiveX controls can only be used as components within other programs, executable ActiveX can be used on its own or called from other projects.

The disadvantage of ActiveX components is that they are operating system dependent. In other words, they only work under the Windows operating system. COM and COM+ are the next generation of Microsoft component development architectures.

Java Beans

Java Beans are the non-Microsoft equivalent of ActiveX. Java Beans components are developed using the Java programming language. The advantage of Java Beans is that they are platform-independent, as is the Java language. The disadvantage is that Java Beans are language-dependent, in other words they can only be written in Java and not in any other language. As a result Java Beans suffer from the slow running speed of Java. The spread of Java Beans and Java Enterprise Beans (JEB) is due to their platform-independence, which makes them ideal for Internet programming, and the increasing importance of Internet programming. It is difficult to cover JEB here but there are several books on the subject, some available and some to be released within the Essential Series.

Common architectures

Common architectures are specifications for software architectures that can be reused. These specifications provide full analysis and design to handle particular problems such as connecting to and carrying transactions on databases in a generic form. In some cases an implementation of these specifications is made available as reusable code. In other words, common architectures can be seen as fully-developed and well-recorded patterns.

One of the most well-known common architectures is CORBA. CORBA is an architecture that provides a solution for distributed databases using object-oriented technology. Several common architectures are being developed especially to facilitate data warehousing. It is worthwhile looking at the Object Management Group (OMG) Web site to see the development of some of these common architectures, most of which are directed towards Internet-based software development.

Managing components

SELECT Enterprise provides extra tools to enable the reuse of components, in the Tools menu (see Figure 16.2). Note the Reuse Component and Publish Component options.

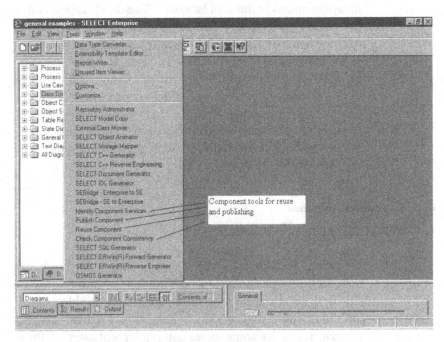

Figure 16.2 Component reuse tools.

Deployment diagrams

A deployment diagram shows how the system is going to be used in the physical world. This diagram is particularly useful during the design of distributed or networked systems where the system may reside or run on different machines. This is especially important in Internet-based systems design, for example.

Experienced designers may often start with this diagram, especially if they have the analysis of the system ready-made from previous experiences. The deployment is often the main difference between one system and another. It is not advisable to start with this diagram unless you have gained significant experience in systems analysis and design.

Deployment diagrams, like component diagrams, are not directly supported by SELECT Enterprise. In fact, most UML books do not provide a precise definition of deployment diagrams. However, we can use general graphics diagrams in SELECT Enterprise to draw deployment diagrams.

Figure 16.3 shows a deployment diagram for a multi-site multi-user database. The diagram was created using the general graphics facility in SELECT Enterprise. The diagram shows two sets of servers: local servers reside in their respective sites, while Web servers may reside in any of the sites, usually in the headquarters of the company. The other thing to notice is that there are administrators, managers and franchised offices. Consider *Office A1;* in this example, what happens in one branch of an office can be reapplied to others. This may not be always the case in deploying systems.

In each branch, users will have direct access to their local servers. However, they will access Web servers through administrators. In other words, the administrators have to give access permission.

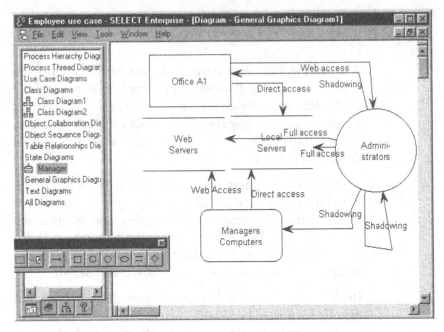

Figure 16.3 *Deploying a database in a multi-site company.*

The deployment diagram in figure 16.3 is much richer than the deployment diagrams presented in UML literature and documentation. In UML, the deployment diagram is built of boxes and links, as in Figure 16.4. It shows the link between a manager PC and the company Web server, which is one of the types of server that may be used by the company branches.

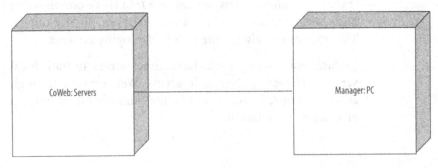

Figure 16.4 *A deployment diagram in UML format.*

Examples

Introduction

This chapter gives examples of analysis and design. We start with an employee database example. From the requirements analysis, we will realise the extent of this database. To provide a design example, we will take part of the database that is concerned with the security of the system. The focus will be on the login procedures.

You can buy this sort of system off the shelf, but it is likely to need customization, which you only get if you design and build the software yourself. In many cases it is useful to have your requirements analyzed to determine which software is suitable for your needs. In other words, what we have learned in this book and what we will practice in this chapter is useful for both software developers and IT managers.

Employee database

The first example we will look at is a simple employee database. You may have a small business and you would like to keep a database about your employees.

The first question to answer is what do you need to know about these employees? The answer for this question will vary depending on the type of business you run. Let us assume that you have four distinct groups in your company:

- Directors
- Staff in the Personnel department
- Administrators
- Other employees

Let us assume that *other employees* do not require access to the database but that the other groups of employees will use the database. We need to save data about employees and users. The first step in identifying the data is to gather and analyze requirements. These requirements will be in two forms:

- Functional requirements: this includes what the system should do, such as retrieving data on employees, sorting by name, adding new employees, and so on.
- Non-functional requirements: for simplification we will consider all requirements that are not functional to be non-functional. This includes what the screens look like, which data is to be saved, security requirements, and so on.

Requirements analysis using use cases

Let us list the requirements for the simple employee database. The best way to do this is to define the data to be maintained, the roles of users and their level of access. The employee database needs to maintain the following data:

- Employees' personal data
- Employees' employment data
- User and access level data.

The roles of users and their level of access are:

- Managers: need full access, especially to employment data
- Personnel department head: needs full access to the data
- Personnel department staff: need read access to most of the data
- System administrators (usually the IT department manager): need full access to both data and system administration tools.

Figure 17.1 shows the use cases that represent the options that managers need to operate the system.

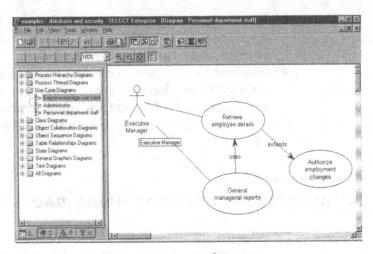

Figure 17.1 Use cases for managers.

Figure 17.2 shows the use cases that represent the options that administrators need to operate the system.

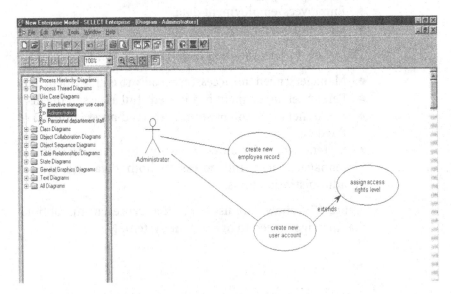

Figure 17.2 Use cases for administrators.

Figure 17.3 shows the use cases that represent the options that the staff and head of the Personnel department need.

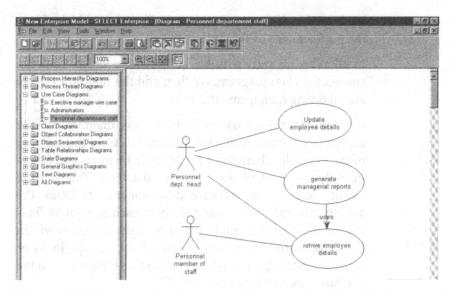

Figure 17.3 Use cases for Personnel department staff and head.

Class identification

Identifying classes is usually the most difficult task in systems analysis and design. There are several ways to make this task easier than it first appears.

If the system being analyzed is a database or is data-centred, we may start from the data and build up towards the classes. This technique is helpful in some cases where the data clearly dominates the system. As an example, consider that we are building a simple stock control program where the operational functions required are *add*, *delete* and *update*. This program is clearly data-centred. In addition, this technique is easier to use if you are experienced in database design and moving towards object-oriented design.

The alternative method, which I prefer, is to start from classes using the minimalism concept and to add properties and methods as required. This technique relies on simplification and the ability to merge classes if necessary. You have to consider the trade-off between the number of classes, the loading of each class and the size of the system, which affects the performance of the system.

In all cases we start with business classes, which form the conceptual class diagram. We then add the interface classes and database management classes.

It would be a big task to build a class diagram for the employee database, which would divert us from the purpose of the example. Therefore I am going to focus on and follow up only one part of the employee database. This is what usually happens in software development: we break the system into sub-systems and develop each separately. This may be done by different teams or different designers within the same team. The system, I have chosen is the login or security system part of which is shown in Figure 17.2 in the use case "Create new user account".

Security system

The security system can be seen as a sub-system of the employee database that gives us a more manageable example. We need to maintain the login information of the users. This requires a database, as with the previous example. In fact we can see this system as a sub-system or stand-alone component that can be used in the employee database to define access level. However, there is a very simple interface, the login window. This means we could use a two-tiered system architecture with a centralized control approach.

Requirements analysis using use cases

The requirements of this system are:
- Maintaining a database of users
- Defining the access level for each user
- Saving session activities when the user logs out.

To maintain such a database of users, we need two main functions: account administration and session administration. Figure 17.4 shows the two use cases.

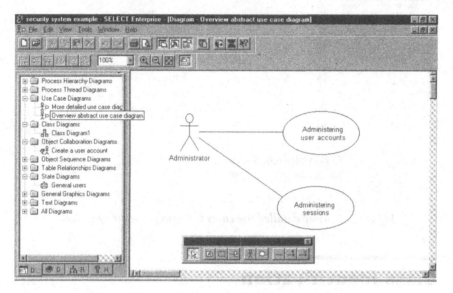

Figure 17.4 Use cases for a simple security system.

If we move from these abstract use cases to more detailed use cases, on the way to achieving real use cases, we have to consider the following functions:

- Creating a new user account
- Updating a user account
- Closing a user account
- Suspending a user account
- Defining and updating access levels
- Logging session activities

Figure 17.5 shows the new use cases. The level of detail usually depends on the technical knowledge of the users we are working with and our own experience with the type of system we are trying to build.

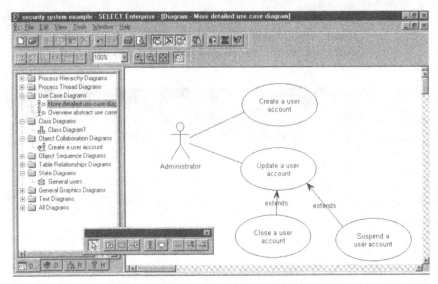

Figure 17.5 More detailed use cases for a simple security system.

Class identification

The classes required for this system are few (see Figure 17.6).

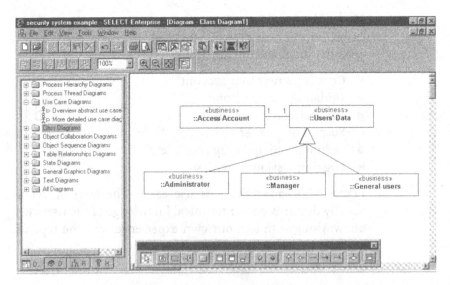

Figure 17.6 A class diagram for a simple security system.

The choice of these classes comes from the use cases and the requirements of the system. At first glance, we may decide there is only one main class required, that is the user account, which can then include all the user data, login and any other data to be held about the account. Figure 17.7 shows the class diagram with interface classes added.

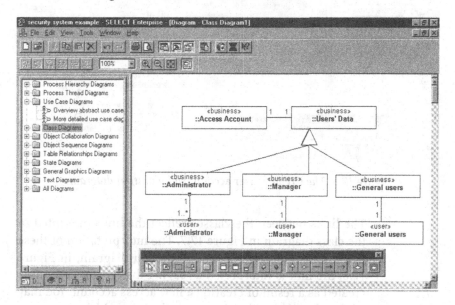

Figure 17.7 The class diagram with interface classes.

Modelling interaction

Now we extend the analysis models further into design models. The interaction between different parts of a package or sub-system is an important aspect of the system. We can model this interaction using collaboration and sequence diagrams. For this system we are going to use a collaboration diagram, which is usually built on use cases.

Figure 17.8 shows the collaboration diagram for the *Create a user account* use case. There are three classes involved in the use case: the *Administrator* interface class, the *Access account* class, and the *General users* class.

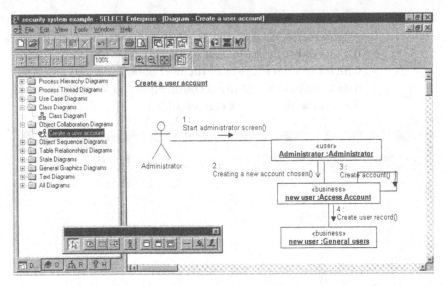

Figure 17.8 *The* Create a user account *collaboration diagram.*

The links between the classes reflect the links presented in the class diagram in Figure 17.7. The interpretation of these links is the objective of the interaction diagram; in Figure 17.8, the link is interpreted as saying that a user account is created as a result of creating a new access account. You may prefer the alternative interpretation, in which an access account is created from user account. In this case, there is no single perfect answer; we must select the best answer depending on what we want to do. All design decisions should be supported by a strong argument. The argument here is based on two factors:

- I want to ensure that each user account has an access account that controls the limits of user access to the system. In other words, no user may exist in our database unless its access privileges have been defined. In effect, we are establishing an integrity constraint between the access account and the user account. If we delete the access account, its associated user account should be deleted too.

- I want to separate the login database from other accounts that may exist in the system. For example there may be an employee share option account to which an employee may have full access privileges unlike the login account of the same employee.

Modelling behaviour

Another important design activity is modelling class behaviour. Modelling behaviour is concerned with designing the class. In traditional software development, this represents the breaking of a program into procedures and functions. If we are implementing the system using an object-oriented programming language, such as Java, the base program unit is the class, which consists of code and encapsulated data.

Figure 17.9 shows a state diagram for the *General users* class (from Figure 17.7). This state diagram shows the behaviour of the class after it has been created and added to the database. When we develop behaviour models, we have to be careful to focus on the behaviour of the class under scrutiny and not confuse it with the classes that instantiate objects of this class. As a result, Figure 17.9 shows the behaviour of *General user* objects. The starting point is for the user to log in. The object has the responsibility for checking the login details and initiating the user session.

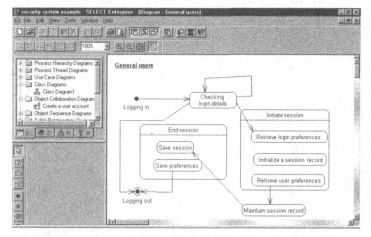

Figure 17.9 A state diagram of the General users *class.*

Note that in Figure 17.9 there is a reference to session recording. There is nothing in our class diagrams in Figures 17.6 and 17.7 about session recording. Do you need a session class to be responsible for recording and maintaining session records? Yes, you do. This is an example of how the object-oriented analysis and design is a recursive procedure. It is worth mentioning here that you may decide to make an existing class, for example the *General users* class, responsible for recording session data. This is a reasonable decision to make if each class has different types of sessions and we want to minimize the number of classes. In this particular example, if we assign a different session class to each user, no extra objects will be instantiated. In other words, the design may become more complicated but the performance of our system will not be affected. Try to draw the class diagram with a *Session* class in both ways and study the effect of the extra number of objects that are created if you have 100 general users, 100 administrators, and 100 managers.

What's Next?

By experience of overall, however, once you have mastered UML standards, it is natural to want to understand and exploit the very many constructs that do justify what you want. Throughout these chapters I have tried to give you a short overview of each notation, giving each a unique meaning as they occur in common usage. However, there is much more to learn about them.

Introduction

This book establishes the basics you need to understand and use UML for fast software design and development. However, UML as a standard modelling language goes much further than the scope of this book. In this chapter we will look at:

- Extensions of UML.
- Real-time UML.

Extensions of UML

Extensions of UML come as a result of shortcomings found by experienced practitioners. Once you have mastered UML standards, it is natural to want to extend and adapt the standards' capabilities to do exactly what you want. In practice, we will find ourselves drawn towards shortcuts. This is usually an acceptable practice as long as everyone within the development team is familiar with these shortcuts.

The nature of the system under development may also affect the way we use UML. The need to handle relational databases may lead us to use entity relationship diagrams as part of our modelling. The system architecture may be developed as free graphics. In addition, some techniques of soft computing analysis and design, such as rich pictures, may be used in place of use cases. Indeed the development team must feel free to break away from the standards and to react to the requirements and circumstances under which the system is developed.

In addition to these non-standard extensions, there are extensions that are being built into newer versions of UML (the current version of UML is 1.3). These extensions do not necessarily add new models or components to the UML standards but may extend existing UML models to enable richer modelling. One of these extensions is real-time UML, which allows the use of UML to model real-time systems.

Real-time UML

Real-time UML is one of the hot subjects in system modelling for use with both embedded and real-time applications. Many real-time systems developers are concerned about the implications of using the OO approach. Their concern comes from the critical time factor and processing required especially if many objects are in use.

Embedded systems, however, seem to be ideal candidates for object-oriented development. Embedded objects are the subject of current active research especially related to areas such as intelligent buildings and new generations of mobile phone networks. There is also a strong link between embedded objects and intelligent agents.

It is worth mentioning here that UML models may be used for the analysis and design of real-time systems even though the implementation does not follow OO programming. It is very similar to modelling databases and implementing them as relational databases.

What is next?

As we get to the end of this book, we have covered the main principles and concepts of both object-oriented modelling and the Unified Modeling Language. What you have learned here will enable you to venture into current advances in object-oriented analysis and design and benefit from them. The next step is to start this venture now through Web sites, books and practical experience. There are several resources provided in Appendix A.

Appendix A

Introduction

This appendix contains some useful web links and book references. The world of software development is fast changing and growing. Depending on your job, you may have to keep up with the new advances in software engineering as it changes in response to new technologies such as the Internet, WAP, mobile devices and so on.

Web resources

- Object Management Group: www.omg.org
- Component Source: www.componentsource.com
- SELECT: www.selectst.com

Book references

Booch, G. *Object Oriented Analysis and Design with Applications*, 2nd Ed. Benjamin Cummins, 1993.

Coad, P. *Object Models: Strategies, Patterns, and Applications.* Prentice Hall (Yourdon Press), 1995.

Coad, P. and Yourdon, E. *Object Oriented Analysis.* Prentice Hall (Yourdon Press), 1991.

Jacobson, I, Christerson, M, Jonsson, PM, Overgaard, G. *Object Oriented Software Engineering: A Use Case Driven Approach.* Addison Wesley, 1992.

Jacobson, I, Ericcson, M, Jacobson, A. *The Object Advantage: Business Process Re-engineering with Object Technology.* Addison Wesley, 1994.

Lorenz, M. *Object Oriented Software Development: A Practical Guide.* Prentice Hall, NJ, 1993.

Pree, W. *Design Patterns for Object Oriented Software Development.* Addison Wesley, 1995.

Wirfs Brock, R, Wilkerson, B, Wiener, L. *Designing Object Oriented Software.* Prentice Hall, 1991.

Yourdon, EN, Whitehead, K, Thomann, J, Oppel, K, Nevermann, P. *Mainstream Objects: An Analysis and Design Approach for Business.* Prentice Hall (Yourdon Press), 1995.

Appendix B

Use cases

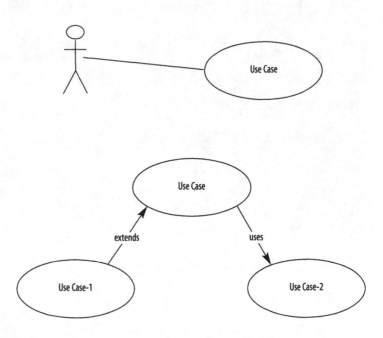

Class diagrams

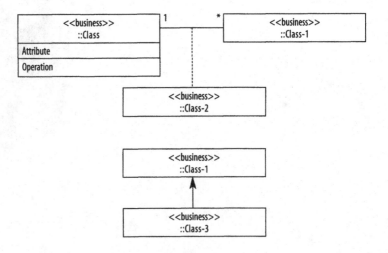

Collaboration diagrams

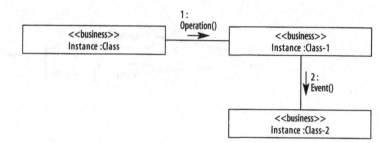

Sequence diagrams

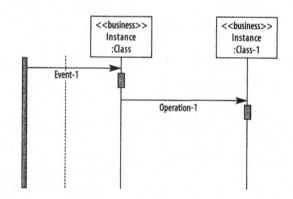

State diagrams

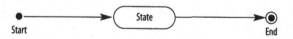

Activity diagrams

Index

Essential VB .NET
fast

John Cowell

Essential VB .NET *fast* is one of the first books available on the latest version of VB .NET. It covers the development environment, the key controls, and the VB programming language including the new additions which allow object oriented programming.

John Cowell describes:
- How to develop both Window and ASP.NET applications with the XP operating system and a Windows 2000 server;
- The development of Windows database applications;
- The development of new controls – to get the reader up and running *fast* with VB .NET.

Using plenty of examples and illustrations, it shows readers the key elements and encourages program development as early as possible ¬ so readers only have to read a few pages before writing programs for themselves.

260 pages
Softcover
ISBN: 1-85233-591-2

Available at bookshops nationwide or from Springer-Verlag directly by contacting +44 (0) 1483 418822